SUCCESS BEHAVIORS OF HIGHLY TALENTED MANAGERS

SUCCESS BEHAVIORS OF HIGHLY TALENTED MANAGERS

WHAT GREAT MANAGERS ACTUALLY DO

Tim McManus

iUniverse, Inc.
New York Lincoln Shanghai

SUCCESS BEHAVIORS OF HIGHLY TALENTED MANAGERS
WHAT GREAT MANAGERS ACTUALLY DO

iUniverse books may be ordered through booksellers or by contacting:

iUniverse
2021 Pine Lake Road, Suite 100
Lincoln, NE 68512
www.iuniverse.com
1-800-Authors (1-800-288-4677)

ISBN-13: 978-0-595-36740-5 (pbk)
ISBN-13: 978-0-595-81160-1 (ebk)
ISBN-10: 0-595-36740-2 (pbk)
ISBN-10: 0-595-81160-4 (ebk)

Printed in the United States of America

To Jan and Nancee, the two best people I know

Contents

SECTION 3: SUMMARIES AND MODELS

INTRODUCTION

What a great job I have. For over 20 years, I have had the privilege of working with thousands of managers, many of whom are great leaders. I really enjoy watching them grow and develop.

Working with these managers is my first love. My second is researching the current trends of leadership and applying them to the behaviors of real managers, and that is what this book is all about.

Many of the leadership theories have really applied to the masses of managers, but one stands out, Emotional Intelligence. After reading books by Daniel Goleman, Hendrie Weisinger, and Peter Cooper, after reviewing the research on the Internet, and after studying the research of the Hay Group, I was convinced there was something to this emotional intelligence thing. So I put it to the test. I started writing down thoughts on how emotionally intelligent behaviors fit into the everyday duties and responsibilities of a manager. And you know what? Emotional Intelligence really does correlate with the successful behaviors of talented managers. Emotional Intelligence actually is the core of what great managers do on a daily basis. The more I wrote, the more I was convinced that emotional intelligence is the real deal.

The writings turned into chapters, and I had them printed, and used as handouts in my leadership programs. A few of the managers encouraged me to get them published, and so I did.

The book is divided into 3 sections:

Section 1:	Chapters 1 and 2 focus on the basics of Emotional Intelligence and how they fit into the theme of leadership.
Section 2:	Chapters 3 through 21 focus on the specific duties and responsibilities of managers, and the emotionally intelligent behaviors needed to be successful.
Section 3:	Chapters 22 and 23 summarize the key ideas in the book. Chapter 22 is a bulleted summary of the behaviors from each chapter (busy managers often need the short version). Chapter 23 is my version of an Emotional Intelligence Model.

It's not necessary to read the book in order, since each chapter is independent of the others. Just pick a topic you like.

Leadership is all about helping people to be extraordinary. To help them accomplish their dreams. It's all about having the courage to connect with people. It's all about relationships.

Think about yourself and the legacy you want to leave. If the legacy is about the people you lead, then read on. You can become an emotionally intelligent manager and, if you do, you have a shot at being a real leader.

All the best.

SECTION 1: LEADING OTHERS

1

EMOTIONAL INTELLIGENCE

IQ AND EQ

Thanks to Dan Goleman and his book, *Emotional Intelligence*, there is tremendous interest, especially among managers, on what Emotional Intelligence means in the workplace. Goleman was not the first to bring this term to life, but he certainly popularized it.

Research indicates that a certain level of IQ and technical knowledge is undoubtedly important in the workplace, but the real differential for managerial success is Emotional Intelligence (EQ). And unlike IQ, which is basically the same throughout your life, EQ competencies can be learned throughout your life.

Goleman's theme is that between 75% and 90% of effective managerial behavior is attributable to Emotional Intelligence. He defines it as:

> *The capacity for recognizing our own feelings and those of others, for motivating ourselves, and for managing emotions well in ourselves and in our relationships.*[1]

Like other experts such as Peter Salovey and John Mayer, Goleman has expanded from a simple definition, and identified key competencies that are applicable to Emotional Intelligence. While competency models may differ, they do have a number of themes in common. Let's look at five of them:

- You need to be aware of and have an accurate assessment of your emotions.

- You need to build your self-confidence.

- You need to work on your self-control.

- You need to be empathetic.

- You need to be able to influence others through excellent communication skills.

Think about how effective you would be if you had these five competencies. On the other hand think about that bulldozing, self-centered boss, you know the one that drives you crazy. Managers who behave in this way are definitely lacking when it comes to the five competencies above, and will rarely be able to build the trust and teamwork that leads to extraordinary success. As a matter of fact, their lack of impulse control will probably lead to their derailment. The proper understanding of how we manage our emotions is critical to our success.

We all know exceptional managers. Maybe they are real smart, but mostly they are known for they ability to relate. I will bet you would say they have a big heart. Maybe EQ is the key to their success.

Before you buy in, let's look at what some of the experts on leadership say to see if their research fits into the Emotional Intelligence theme.

NOEL TICHY

Noel Tichy is currently a professor at the University of Michigan. His expertise on leadership has been developed by many practical and academic ventures. He worked closely with Jack Welch at General Electric in developing the renowned Crotonville training facility. He is an outstanding author, and his book, *The Leadership Engine,* is one of the best books on leadership you can find.

One of the main concepts in his book is that leaders train other leaders and to do this they need to have a teachable point of view. The following quote from his book has Emotional Intelligence written all over it.

"To influence and lead, one needs teachable points of view not only in the form of teachable ideas and values themselves, but also in how to nurture and develop good ideas and strong values in others. In Chapter 9, I will talk about how the very best leaders personalize these points of view and spin them out as stories that engage followers emotionally as well as intellectually. But the point I want to make is that great leaders are great teachers not only because they know what they think, but also because they take the time to organize their thoughts in ways they can communicate them clearly." [2]

The themes of self-awareness, self-confidence, empathy, and influence are evident in this short paragraph, and there is plenty of evidence of Emotional Intelligence throughout his book.

WARREN BENNIS

Of all the authors on Leadership, Warren Bennis is one of the most prolific. His research is solid and ongoing. In his book, *Leaders,* which he authored with Burt Nanus, he identified the importance of having a positive self-regard:

"Positive self-regard is related to maturity, but we'd prefer the term 'emotional wisdom' to maturity. Maturity sounds too much like the point where one outgrows childish behavior. But our leaders seemed to retain many of the positive characteristics of the child: enthusiasm for people, spontaneity, imagination, and an unlimited capacity to learn new behavior. Emotional wisdom, as we've come to understand it, reflects itself in the way people relate to others." [3]

The EQ competencies of self-awareness, self-control, empathy, communication, and influence clearly stand out in this statement.

JAY CONGER

As a former head of the University of Southern California's Leadership Institute, Jay Conger is on the cutting edge of leadership. In his book, *Winning 'Em Over,* he talks about the importance of connecting emotionally:

> "In research that I have conducted on business leaders, I found that the most effective leaders draw upon their emotions to generate commitment. They understand that the heart and the soul are often far more potent energizers than the head. Aristotle himself believed strongly in the emotional engagement of an audience as a critical factor in persuasion. A persuader's appeal must convey his own commitment and touch a chord of feelings with his audience. We can accomplish this by sharing sincere feelings that mirror the desires, needs, hopes, fears, dreams and values of those whom we are persuading." [4]

JAMES KOUZES & BARRY POSNER

Kouzes and Posner's book, *The Leadership Challenge,* is one of the all time best sellers of business books. They have identified the practices that help people to do the extraordinary. Their thoughts on when leaders felt their proudest are interesting:

> "Traditional management teaches that leaders ought to be cool, aloof, and analytical: they ought to separate emotion from work. Yet when real life leaders discuss what they're the most proud of in their own careers, they describe feelings of inspiration, passion elation, intensity, challenge, caring and kindness—and yes, even love." [5]

MORGAN MC CALL

Morgan McCall has done extensive research on the development of leaders. He has studied not only the stories of great success, but also the stories of great derailment. In his book, *High Flyers,* he talks about people who have derailed:

> "Whether failing to listen to advice and feedback, refusing to change when change was needed, behaving in ways that alienated other people or some other act of self-destruction, individuals that derailed always played a significant role in their own demise…Because those who derailed were

often unaware of their own role or actively denied it, they could be described as conspirators in their own misfortune." [6]

Self-awareness is so critical to your success.

WHAT ABOUT YOU

We could go on and on citing the research, but I think we have enough. The research on the importance of Emotional Intelligence is getting richer every day. When it comes to excelling, we all have enough IQ, or we wouldn't be succeeding. It's the EQ that will make the difference; it's the EQ that will help us become a better leader.

Here are ten things you should consider to help you with your own EQ.

1. Self-awareness is the real key to emotional intelligence. Are you aware of how people you work with view your behavior? Take some time to do some non-judgmental awareness of how you behave. Now being non-judgmental is not easy, we are constantly judging everything. But try. Pay particular attention to how you are behaving, especially in stressful situations.

2. Now let's be judgmental. What was good? What are you doing that alienates others? Why? What could you have done better? What were the implications of your behavior?

3. Are you open to feedback, or do you close down and get defensive when others give you feedback and criticism? You need candid feedback if you are to grow and learn. Accept it, want it, and ask for it.

4. Are you able to anticipate how your words or actions will impact others? Do you frame things so that others are receptive, or do you find that you are antagonizing others? Why?

5. Are you able to respond calmly during stressful times? Do you regularly fly off the handle? Do you show restraint? Are you able to calm others? Why?

6. Do you listen well? Can you see things from the other person's point of view? Are you constantly pushing your own agenda without taking the time to think of how it will affect others?

7. Can you show vulnerability? Do you admit when you make a mistake? Do you take credit for others ideas and work?

8. Do you follow through on your promises?

9. Do you set high goals for yourself and others? Do you believe in others? Do you encourage others?

10. Are you brutally candid with yourself? Do you forgive yourself?

These ten ideas/questions will help you get started on your way to becoming more emotionally intelligent.

2

LEADERSHIP

VINCE LOMBARDI

Willie Davis is a remarkable person. As the first member of his family ever to attend college, he graduated with a major in Industrial Arts and a minor in Math. He also played a little football for the legendary Grambling coach, Eddie Robinson. He ran several companies and sat on the Board of Directors on a number of other companies. In between he managed to put in a Hall of Fame career with the Green Bay Packers.

When an extraordinary person like Willie talks about the leaders who have influenced him, you really need to listen. I once heard Willie talk about the fabled Vince Lombardi and the impact Lombardi had not only on Willie, but also on all the players on the Green Bay team. His words about how Lombardi made him feel are extremely powerful. What I heard him say was:

"He made me feel important. He made me feel wanted."

These two simple sentences summarize what leadership is all about. Leadership is all about emotion and heart. It's about caring first. Sure you must be competent and smart, but if you don't care, you will not lead.

You can be strong and tough, but you must care about people, and they must know you really care about them. You can't fake it. A major study conducted at the Center for Creative Leadership found that insensitivity to others is a major factor in the derailment of managers.

This caring stuff is tough work. You see things through your own filters, and you see things differently from anyone else on the planet. To care enough to see things from another person's point of view, to see things through their filters, their values and their fears—this is what real caring is all about.

YOGI BERRA

Yogi Berra has been quoted and misquoted as much as anyone in our country today. One saying attributed to him is:

"You can observe a lot by watching."

You know what? He was right. You **can** observe a lot by watching. Leaders are more aware than others are. They know what is going on around them. They are out observing, and, as a result, they are out learning, not guessing, about the reality of their particular situation. Is your awareness level high? Are you observant?

RESPECT

Caring starts with treating people with a belief in people and their potential. It starts with treating people with respect.

Don't you just hate the term "subordinate?" Do you like being called a subordinate? Many managers think that the people working for them are subordinates and should be happy that they have a job. They think of subordinates as tools to get the work out. They have a need to keep complete control, and they do. As a result, they exhibit little respect for the people working for them.

In the 1960's, organizations got larger and larger, and control and management were very important. There was a need for managers to manage the growing functions of business. But today, business needs to get smaller and closer to the customer. And in this environment of change, leadership is more critical. And leadership starts with respecting the worth, capability and potential of each follower, not by treating people as subordinates.

The golden rule is always a good one: "Treat people the way you want to be treated." The problem is that the golden rule has gotten tougher. Today it reads: "Treat people the way they always wanted to be treated, but never were." Check yourself often. Are you hiring great people, and treating them with the highest degree of respect?

It's tough to treat people the way they always want to be treated. Don't you just love the famous quote: "Walk in the other's shoes for a mile." Oh, really. Would you like to walk in my old shoes for a mile? As comfortable as they are to me, they would be just as uncomfortable to you. My values, dreams and goals are probably different from yours. I come from a different point of view. And yet, as a leader, it is important for you to work to understand where I am coming from, and that is what respect is really all about.

Are you aware of how your emotions and behaviors are affecting how your followers view you? Do they know that you respect them? In order to gain respect you must give respect.

WALT DISNEY

Walt Disney was known to have said: "If you can dream it, you can do it." As one of the great dreamers of our time, Disney had an inordinate amount of incredible accomplishments.

Disney dreamt about possibilities, about what could be, not about what is. Most of us get caught up in the past, and we think things will remain basically as they are. Dreamers think in the future and have a vision of what can be done.

Research on leadership emphasizes the importance of vision, and vision starts with dreams. You need to be able to develop a vision that is meaningful if you truly want to lead.

Think about how things have changed over the past few years. Think about the realities of today. Spend at least two hours a week thinking about the way things are going to be. The Internet has changed everything, and leaders must be on top of what the changes mean to their team. Keep a notebook just to jot down ideas on where you see things going, and why you think this way. Don't limit yourself. Just jot down what you think may be possible.

Building a vision is an ongoing task. Never stop dreaming. Keep a notebook and write down thoughts about what you see your team accomplishing. Keep reviewing your notes and continue to put your thoughts into writing until a vision starts forming in your mind. And once you have a vision that you are satisfied with, share it with others; ask them to improve it. Incorporate any of their thoughts that you think improve your vision. And once you have a vision, you must communicate it to your team over and over again. And no matter how clear the vision is to you, it is always a work in progress; it is never complete. Even a great vision should, not could, be improved upon.

A key component to any great vision is that it is moral and meets the needs and values of its followers. Hitler's vision for Germany met the needs and values of many of the German people, but it was flawed because of its lack of morality, and in the long run it was rejected.

Visions, like dreams, are often remarkably simple, but they are always powerful. One caveat about visions: I'm not saying you have to be a "visionary" to be a leader, but you need to have a clear vision of where you want your team to go and what you want them to accomplish. You may already be on the right road, and there may be no need to change. Just make sure you keep your eyes wide open as to the realities and possibilities surrounding you. Building a vision requires that you remain awake to the challenges and opportunities that your team will encounter.

COURAGE

Dr. Martin Luther King, Jr. had the courage to work to change people with a strong vision of what civil rights really meant. Mother Theresa had the courage to work her vision of helping the poorest of the poor live a valued life. Nelson Mandela had the courage to spend decades in prison fighting for the rights of his people. We could go on and on talking about great leaders, and we would find that they all lived their dream, mainly because they were all courageous.

Leadership is an activity, not a position. Leaders can come from anywhere. One thing they will have in common is that they have a vision that is filled with possibilities. But the vision is just a guide; courage to act on a vision makes it a reality.

Courage is as much about not doing something as it is about doing something. Dr. King knew there was a time to march, but there were also times to cut a march short. Courage combined with good judgment is a powerful leadership theme. Foolish courage is rarely effective.

It takes courage to fight for your people. It takes courage to give them solid and honest feedback. It takes courage to help someone get a deserved promotion when they are doing a great job for you, but your company has put a freeze on promotions and pay increases. It takes courage to give others credit when nobody is giving you any. It takes courage to trust and be trusted. It takes courage to admit when you're wrong.

AWARENESS

So much of leadership is about adapting to the pressures and circumstances of the moment at hand. Leaders who handle situations the best are intuitive and much more aware of what is taking place around them.

Mohandas Gandhi earned his leadership authority because he was closer to the Indian people than anyone. He lived the life of poverty that they lived. He experienced the prejudice that they did. He understood the strengths and weaknesses of the Indian culture better than anyone. His awareness, coupled with his vision and courage, helped him become a model of leadership.

All too often, someone who was an outstanding leader in a smaller job is promoted and, to the surprise of many, becomes distant. He or she loses touch with the grassroots and, as a result, is much less aware of the reality that going on around them.

That is the primary reason why many CEO's, people with a "leadership position," are not always viewed as real leaders. They lose touch, and they are less aware of what is really is going on in their organization. The only time you see them out with the troops is when they are making a speech, or accepting some accolade, or giving someone they have never met a deserved award.

Be careful. Things get done at the grassroots level. Never lose touch. The key to being "street smart" is to be out in the streets.

POSITIVE

It's not much fun being around the sulkers and negativity coordinators. It's a lot easier to be around someone who is optimistic about the possibilities that are in front of them. A positive person often surrounds him or herself with other positive people.

It's easy to get caught up with negative thoughts. It seems like people are more comfortable talking about what's wrong with work, or what's wrong with other people. It seems that it is more fun gossiping than it is to talk about all the great things that are happening around us.

Don't get involved with the negative gossip, and never talk negatively about any of your people, unless you are about to fire them. Even then, be careful about saying negative things. If you say bad things about one person, other people will wonder if you will say bad things about them. Saying bad things about people is not a good way to build an atmosphere of trust and respect. When in doubt, be positive.

You know it's tough to be positive when the negatives seem to be so reasonable, but you must.

MOMENTUM

Momentum toward mediocrity has been staggering. Staying with the status quo is a form of momentum, a momentum that leads to greater bureaucracy, greater comfort and misleading results. It's like the winning sports team who opens up a big lead, but for some reason changes their strategy and starts protecting their lead. The other team starts getting a few breaks, and before you know it the momentum changes. You know what happens next; the other team wins. Everyone wonders how such a collapse can happen in such a short period of time. The reason: momentum

Leaders recognize the power of momentum. They do everything they can to focus on what is driving the organization forward. They are aware of the competition, the marketplace, the psychographics as well as the demographics, and they recognize real results versus results that happen because of timing and luck.

Watch your own team. What is the momentum like? Talk to them about getting better all the time. Talk to your "players" about ways they can support each other. Ask for advice and help, don't go it alone. If you can get your team thinking and acting in a positive manner, momentum will likely take over.

FOCUS

What gets focused on gets done. What are you focused on, and is it aligned with what your team is focused on? Are you and your team clearly focused on a mutually defined vision, and do you challenge the vision to ensure that it remains viable and current?

If you are disciplined enough to focus on your vision, and really spend your time acting in ways that will make the vision a reality, then your actions will match your words. Nothing is worse than you not "walking the talk."

CHANGE

Leadership is all about change. Things just don't stand still, but many organizations and teams seem to be stuck in quicksand. Change has always been part of business, but the messiness and complexity of change today is just a reminder of what is to come. Will you be able to handle the changes ahead? If you are a leader, you will.

Change has quite a few parts; let's look at some.

* Most people are quite happy and comfortable doing things the way they are doing them. You are probably comfortable with the way you do things and are reluctant to change. To get people to change, you must disrupt this comfort level.

* Individuals resist change, even positive change. Just think about how hard it is to stick to a diet that you know is good for you.

* A company's history and culture are powerful drivers of the current status quo. It's easy for people to fall back on the old ways of doing things when the transition to the new is painful.

* Even when people understand the benefits to change, getting to the mind is not enough. Change is about the mind and the heart. Change has a lot to do with emotion.

* People desire to have control and ownership in what they do. Change is a disruption in control and ownership.

* Change can be undermined and stopped at many different levels. Change requires buy-in from every level that is going to be affected by the change.

* Maintaining the change requires constant attention.

* Change requires that people give it a fair portion of their time. It's tough for people to give the proper level of urgency to something new, different, and often painful

There are many reasons why change is necessary, and why leadership is so important. Leaders can influence people to do things differently. Leaders are focused on getting results through people, and results often mean changing from the status quo. Let's compare leaders with non-leaders as they relate to change.

LEADERS	NON-LEADERS
Leaders build a vision centered around dreams and possibilities, while keeping a keen awareness of the realities of the work environment.	Non-leaders work to extend the status quo.
Leaders encourage two-way open communication. They listen.	Non-leaders dictate. They tell people what to do. They are selective listeners.
Leaders understand that not everyone will buy into their vision. They invite dissent, candid dissent.	Non-leaders only want to hear the good stuff. They discourage dissent.
Leaders are confident and self-assured, but they never let their ego get in the way.	Non-leaders like status and often let their ego stand out.

Leaders understand that getting people to change is not easy, and they understand and respect the pain that is involved. Non-leaders think that all they need to do to initiate change is make powerful statements about the upcoming change. However nothing could be further from the truth.

If you are going to lead change, you must be willing to work in a messy environment: an environment that is full of discomfort and disruption…an environment that is full of resistance and reluctance…an environment where adaptability and flexibility replace predictability.

Your greatest challenge will be to have the energy to stay the course, to build a coalition of key influencers throughout the organization who support and, more importantly, are committed to the change. You will need to go with little tangible hard evidence that the change will benefit the people who will work the change. You will have to constantly communicate the vision of what is possible, and support the vision with every small, or big, win that comes along. You must be willing to take the heat when people are taking shots, and saying we need to go back to the way we always do things.

Change is part of life, and is accelerating at a rate faster than ever before. Leaders understand human behavior and help their followers absorb change at a rate they can handle.

EGO

Leaders have a solid sense of self worth, and most of them have a lot of confidence; some are even egotistical. You have to feel good about yourself to lead. A little dose of ego is necessary, but keep it in check. Very few people willingly follow someone who is always promoting himself or herself.

DERAILMENT

There are many stories about successful people who don't live up to their leadership potential and see their career cut short. Here are a few reasons why potential leaders derail along the way:

- Insensitivity—Leadership is an earned role, and your followers will be your greatest admirers or your greatest detractors. Don't underestimate their power. They can make or break you, and they tend to break those who are insensitive to their needs.

- Arrogance—You usually get to a leadership position because you are good at what you do. Be careful that you don't allow your success to lead to arrogance. You will not gain by showing your superiority over others.

- Aloofness—Similar to arrogance in many ways is becoming aloof. You lose touch when you become aloof. Now this is not the same as being shy, it is more a sense that others may have that says to them that you think you are too far above them to care about them.

- Rigidity—Today things are changing with such speed that it is the flexible people who succeed. Listen, observe, communicate, but don't fall into the trap of being right all the time.

- Dictatorial—There are many stories of successful autocratic leaders, but more and more people are reacting unfavorably to the over control that is being forced upon them. Humanistic leadership is what works today. Command and control is out. Listening and relationship building is in.

- Looking Good—Derailing managers use defense mechanisms (blaming others, denial, rationalization, scapegoating, etc.) so that they always look good to their bosses. They are users of people. They view their staff as a tool to carry out tasks, not people struggling to reach their dreams.

- No Legacy—After a period of time, leaders can point to people who have grown and have moved to better jobs. The derailing manager tries to hoard talent. They readily talk about their best talent in a negative way so that they are not thought of as superstars. Derailing managers are a roadblock to the talented person. Talent often leaves because they can't get ahead with this manager.

- Hero Worship—Derailing managers spend most of their time pleasing those in power. It's easy to spot these people because they will always latch on to a person of power when they enter a room. They even fool the powerful people for a time because they often have excellent social skills.

- Lack of Integrity—A sure road to failure. Low integrity leads to low trust, and leaders must be trusted. Integrity means that you will do the right and ethical thing even when nobody's looking.

Your followers will make or break you. You need them to exhibit their unique talents to make your workplace a bigger success. Be careful that you don't fall into the traps of derailment, because these same followers can become compliant, unresponsive, unproductive and even destructive. And that is not what leadership is all about.

SO WHAT IS LEADERSHIP?

Leadership is the ability to:

- Move emotions
- Form a vision of possibilities
- Care and be empathetic
- Be positive in the face of real pressure
- See clearly and refocus during messy times
- Communicate and influence
- Dream
- Be aware and awake
- Have the courage to do what's right
- "Walk the talk"

Leaders relish in the challenge to help others achieve greatness. What a challenge. What a responsibility. No wonder there are so few real leaders.

SECTION 2: DUTIES AND RESPONSIBILITES OF SUCCESSFUL MANAGERS

3

HIRING: THE MAKE IT OR BREAK IT SKILL

You may be a superstar, but, if you are leading a team or a group, they are the ones who will make you great. They could also be the ones who bring you down. Never compromise on the people you hire.

PRODUCTIVITY

Every few of years we hear the talk was all about how America is falling behind, how our productivity is lagging, and how foreign competition is taking over. It's popular to focus on the negatives and ignore the positives. Well, we always seem to bounce back, and frankly there is no limit to our future. Sure, there will be ups and downs, recessions and booms, and it is the organizations that have hired the best people and have them working up to their potential that will succeed. But there will be some organizations that lag and fall behind. They will not reach the same levels of productivity that they have in the past, and a large part of the problem will be in the people they can attract and hire.

How great do you want to become? A lot will have to do with the people you choose to help you in your quest. There are a lot of good people just waiting to show their stuff. It's up to you to make sure that you have your share of this talent working with you. Remember; it's the quality of the followers that make a leader great.

Maybe you are one of the lucky ones, and all your people are superstars, but few are so lucky. There is going to be a time when you are going to have to upgrade your team, and, when that time comes you need to be ready with a well-thought-out hiring plan.

WHAT TO LOOK FOR

Every hiring decision you make will affect the way you manage and lead. You need to find strong followers, not just any followers. You need to find followers who really want the job, and are willing and able to do the job well. And so the first thing you must do before you hire anyone is to determine exactly what the job entails and what a great candidate will look like.

Think a lot about skills and qualities that are necessary for a candidate to be successful in this particular job and in this particular culture. Ask your team members for advice on what they think are the critical attributes of a good candidate. Ask your peers and your boss for their view. Collate all the information and come to a firm conclusion of what you are looking for in a good candidate, and then don't compromise by hiring someone who lacks the skills and character you have identified.

FINDING CANDIDATES

Finding candidates is not always easy, and, unless you have a terrific flow of resumes coming across your desk, you will need to be very proactive in your search. Here are a few ideas you may want to use.

* Look around you. Someone on your own team may be a perfect candidate for promotion. Also look around your own company. There are many people doing jobs they are overqualified for, and who would love to move into a more demanding role.

* Ask your best people for referrals. This will be your best source of good candidates. If possible, offer a bonus to any team member who refers a candidate who gets hired. You may want to carry this one step further and give an additional bonus to the team member if the new hire performs at an agreed upon level of performance.

* Put a Blind Ad (an ad with a P.O. Box number instead of your company name) in the Sunday addition of your major newspaper. You will get a lot

of resumes, but only a few gems. A variation of this is to put a phone number in the ad; that is, if you want to return a number of phone calls.

* Hold a career night. Put an ad in the paper three weeks prior to the night, and request that resumes be sent to your office. Screen the resumes and invite the good ones to the career night. Have a good speaker give a brief talk about your company; give each candidate a brief screening interview and conclude with refreshments. You should be able to find a few good candidates to invite in for a formal interview.

(Note: In small towns, career nights are often less effective. A lot of people don't want it getting around that they are looking for a job.)

* Ask new hires, your friends and your clients for referrals.

* If you have the funds, use a respected recruiter. Always take time with recruiters so they know exactly what you are looking for.

* Look at people who do a good job servicing you or your company. Some may be looking for a change. At the very least, they can be a good referral source.

* Use the Internet. There are numerous sites that create matches between job seekers and particular jobs. Be sure to include your e-mail address in any job information you are putting out.

* Call the personnel department of a company that is downsizing. They may have just what you are looking for. Find out who they are using for outsourcing, and follow up to see if they have any candidate for you to consider.

* Talk to the Dean of your local college about setting up an intern program where talented young people can get college credit for real on-the-job training. You in turn will be able to observe, evaluate and recruit some good young talent.

* Check out the library; it has a wealth of information. Ask the librarian for help.

* Join local business clubs. You should meet some impressive people who may fit your needs.

* Contact the Alumni Director and placement office at your local college. They are always ready to help.

THE RESUME

The resume is a good screening tool. The candidate should take care and effort in putting it together.

You should look for two things as you review the resume: achievements and concerns. Achievements such as awards, leadership positions or regular job promotions, are all indications of a potential winner. Concerns such as gaps on the resume, no signs of achievement or excessive job hopping are indications of a potential problem.

Always remember that there is little correlation between the quality of the resume and the quality of the candidate. Credentials can be misleading. Be disciplined and screen out those resumes where there are too many concerns and not enough achievements.

SCREEN

After identifying the key characteristics, and finding some evidence of those characteristics in a candidate's resume, you or another qualified person should do a screening interview.

Let's say that you want to hire above average achievers. An effective screening interview would start with you explaining what the job entails, and giving a clear picture of what a successful candidate will experience on a daily basis. Then ask a pointed question such as:

> "I am looking for people with a lot of achievement to help make our company even more successful. For the next 15 minutes or so I would like you to brag about your achievements. Tell me about accomplishments, things in your life that you are most proud of, and why you are proud of them."

Sit back and listen. You will find out very quickly if the candidate meets your key characteristic; in this case, achievement. If the person convinces you that he or she has the basics you are looking for, invite him or her to continue with the hiring process. If applicants don't have what it takes, let them know, but do it with sensitivity.

The next logical step would be a full interview.

THE OPENER

Qualified candidates who have gotten through the screening process should be invited back for an in-depth interview. Having good interviewing skills is crucial, and it all starts with a smooth opener.

The opener is a very important part of the interview and one of the most overlooked. A good opener should put the candidate at ease and set a focused tone on what is going to take place in the next hour or so. Here is an example of a typical opener:

"(Name), thanks for coming in today. What I thought we could do is spend some time talking about you. I will ask you a number of questions about your work and your interests, and then I will leave some time for you to ask me about anything that you need to know—Is that O.K. with you?

Great, let's start with…"

Another example would be:

"(Name) let's review what we will do today. Our goal is to see whether (the position) is best suited to you and your interests. And so I would like to ask you a number of questions about your work, goals, education and hobbies.

Let's start by finding out more about you; then let's turn it around so that you can ask anything you need to know about the job or me. O.K. with you?"

Keep the opener short, and simply review what is going to happen during the interview. It will get the interview off to a smooth start.

TRANSITIONS

Many interviewers like to structure the interview into such specific categories as career interest, work experience, activities, hobbies and education. It helps keep the interviewer focused and on track. If this is the way you like to conduct your interviews, make sure you build in transitions so you can move smoothly into new categories.

An example of a simple transition is:

> "We have reviewed your work experience and education. Now let's take a few minutes to talk about your hobbies. Let's talk about how you relax and have fun. Tell me about…"

Transitions will not only help you; they will help the candidate. They help you both to stay focused and on track.

QUESTIONING TECHNIQUES

If you talk to the experts, they will tell you to use as many open-ended questions as you can, and in theory they are right. But for most of us this is hard advice to follow, mainly because we are so ingrained in the habit of asking closed-ended questions. This practice can be effective when you have a talkative candidate who answers yes and no questions with a twenty-minute discourse. For the most part, though, the experts are right; try to stay with more open questions…but how?

Whenever you find yourself asking such closed questions as—"Can you handle stress?"—you are actually putting yourself in a wonderful position to get the candidate to open up. The reason is that the closed question actually leads to a number of open questions that you can easily layer on top of your original closed question. Here is an example of this questioning sequence:

> Can you handle stress?
> > Tell me about a time you had to work under stress.
> > What did you do?
> > What went well?
> > What would you do differently?
> > Tell me more?
> > Give me another example of a time you were under stress?
> > What did you do?
> > Etc.

By asking sets of questions, you will get to know a lot about the candidate. Always ask the follow-up questions. Ask the who, what, when, where, why and how questions whenever you are at a loss for what questions to ask.

Here are a few great questions you can use as follow-up questions over and over again:

What else?
Tell me more…
What did you like most about…?
What did you like least about…?
What did you accomplish?
What were the setbacks? How did you handle them?
Specifically, what did you do?

CORE QUESTIONS

Having a set of core questions is a good idea. You can always fall back on these questions to give you solid information to evaluate each candidate, and they give you a basic structure to use. This structure is particularly useful when you are in a time bind and don't have time to prepare for the interview. Here are some core questions that help identify key leadership themes: self-esteem, courage, focus, discipline, and achievement.

SELF-ESTEEM

- What do you regard as your best characteristics—the ones that have enabled you to accomplish what you have thus far? Please take some time and don't be afraid to brag.

- What about the other side of the coin? We all have shortcomings—what are the areas you want to improve upon? Why?

- Do you consider yourself to be successful? Why?

- Let's play a role. Play your current boss for a minute. What would Mr./Ms._____ say about you? What will your boss say about you when you resign?

- In summarizing your strengths and weaknesses, why would you be a good prospect for this job?

- How would your friends describe you?

- What are you most proud of?

- Tell me about a responsibility you enjoyed?

- What did you do to meet that responsibility?

ACHIEVEMENT

- Tell me about a competitive situation that you have been involved in. How did you handle the situation? What did you accomplish? How?

- As you look back, what do you consider to be your greatest accomplishment so far? Why was it important? What exactly did you do?

- Give me another example of a good accomplishment?

- What do you think are the characteristics that distinguish true achievers from other people? Tell me about a time when you exhibited those characteristics?

- What's been your greatest responsibility?

- What are your best talents? What makes you a great candidate for this job?

COURAGE

- What are some of the risks you've taken in your life? What were the results?

- What was the most difficult situation you faced? How did you react?

- Tell me about areas you want to improve. What's your plan?

- Give me an example of when you had to handle conflict? What did you do?

- Tell me about a time you failed. What did you learn?

- Give me an example of when you turned around a situation that wasn't going so well.

FOCUS

- Let's talk about your career goals. What are your goals for the next six months? Where do you want to be three years from now?

- What do you think distinguishes a superstar from someone who is average?

- What is your understanding of this job? What would you think would be most challenging? Most rewarding? Least rewarding?

- What would you change about your current job? What are you looking for in this job?

- Why does this job fit your expectations?

- What were your goals for today? What are the most important things that you did today?

DISCIPLINE

- Tell me about your typical day.

- What problems do you usually have in getting things done?

- How do you spend your time when you are not working? Hobbies? Interests? How much time do you get to spend on these?

- What have you done to become better at your current position?

- How do you organize and plan?

LEGAL/ILLEGAL

A caution about questions. Ask job-related questions. Never ask a question in any of the following areas unless it relates directly to a real job requirement:

* Race
* Religion
* Political Beliefs
* Sex
* National Origin
* Physical Disabilities
* Marital Status
* Age
* Arrests
* Childcare Problems

You can ask about:

* Convictions (not arrests)
* Availability to work overtime (if necessary for the job)

* Work Experience
* Authorization to work in the United States

If there is any question as to the validity to any question, don't ask it. There are too many great questions you can ask without having to ask illegal ones.

CANDIDATE TALK

One of the common mistakes interviewers make is to allow the candidate to go off track. What happens is the candidate starts talking about the situation they were in and not what they did in the situation. Although the stories are interesting and the candidates' credentials are impressive, we really didn't find out what the candidate did to earn the credentials. Be careful; don't get caught up in the stories.

It's critical that you get the candidate talking about his or her actual accomplishments, likes, dislikes and results. If you find the candidate going off track, try using this statement:

> "I seem to have gotten us off track. The situation you are describing is very interesting, and what I would like to focus on is what you did. Tell me about how you handled...."

By taking the blame for getting off track, you can easily get the candidate focused without the candidate becoming defensive. It is an easy and effective method, so don't be afraid to use it often.

THE CLOSE

Prepare your close. Many interviewers don't have a plan on how to close and it causes them a lot of time. Keep the close simple and cordial. Thank the candidate and inform him or her on any next step. Here is an example of a simple close:

> "(Name) thanks for coming in today and being candid with me. I will be looking at a few more candidates before making a final evaluation. I will call you (send you a letter) in _____ days to let you know what is happening."

Always try to have the candidate leave with a good impression about you and the company. You always want them to be saying positive things to their friends. Word of mouth is important advertising for your company.

EVALUATION

Immediately after the interview write down, or better yet record, your impressions of the candidate. Here are a few points to consider when evaluating the candidate:

- How was the candidate's impact?
- What was the energy level like during the interview?
- What specific evidence can you point to that this candidate can do the job?
- Does the candidate really want the job? Why?
- Do you feel that the candidate has the potential to grow? Why?
- What bothers you about the candidate?
- How will the candidate fit in with your team?
- Would the candidate impress your customers?
- Would I be pleased to introduce the candidate as my partner?
- Would I want this person working for my competition?

Going a little further. If you are looking for an emotionally intelligent person, consider these questions:

- Does the candidate present himself/herself with self-assurance and confidence?
- Do you feel the candidate was candid?
- Does the candidate handle adversity with a positive attitude and resilience?
- Is the candidate focused when under pressure?
- Can the candidate admit to making mistakes?
- Can the candidate handle difficult decisions with tact?

- Does the candidate hold himself/herself accountable to challenging goals?

- Does the candidate care about others?

- Did the candidate ask good questions?

- Did the candidate keep you interested?

- Does the candidate have a passion for working with others?

- Will the candidate be a positive addition to your team?

Be tough on evaluation. If you have any doubts, think about next steps: a second interview, an interview with another member of the team, or simply deciding to hire or not to hire the candidate.

Multiple interviews with different people are preferable to a single interview, and should give you richer information to evaluate. Team interviews can also be effective since people will pick up different things during the interview. Whatever process you use, make sure that everyone is looking for the same thing, and that everyone is well trained in the interview process.

One final thought about evaluating the candidate. I feel it is important that you like the candidate. If you hire someone who is talented, but someone you don't like, you may spend time helping them get off to a good start, but ignore him or her in the long run. This is a big mistake.

A DOZEN THOUGHTS

1. Don't leave the hiring decisions to someone else. You must be involved.

2. Watch out for initial impressions, both good and bad.

3. Check references when you can.

4. Excuse only the candidate's nervousness during the interview. They should be a little nervous, but should be able to perform well under the stress.

5. Prepare for the interview. Know what you are looking for, and have a plan on how to find it.

6. Conduct interviews in private. It is acceptable to have a second interviewer in the room with you.

7. Try to put the candidate at ease. The best interviews are a conversation, not an inquisition.

8. Listen. The applicant should do most of the talking.

9. Ask personal questions in a natural manner.

10. Keep focused and in control. Direct the candidate in the direction you want to go.

11. Interview during the part of the day when you are at your best. You need to be alert.

12. Keep on an even keel. Don't let the candidate know when you view something as negative. You don't want the candidate closing up on you.

PITFALLS

Let's focus on two pitfalls that can really hurt your hiring process:

1. The early decision.

   Often interviewers make decisions based on first impressions and spend the interview time to confirm their initial reaction. Don't let this happen to you.

   Never compromise on your hiring process. Treat all candidates the same and be careful that you don't play favorites by leading them to the answers you want to hear.

2. Hiring the best available candidate.

   Often the best available candidate is not the talented person you need to achieve the level of success you have identified as your goal. Don't compromise. If you haven't found the right person for the job, go back to the drawing board and start over.

   The best of a bad group may look like a good candidate, but really isn't. Evaluate each candidate with the highest standards in mind. Always be in the hiring mentality. You never know when a great candidate might pop up.

IMPORTANT, BUT

Ask managers what is the most important part of their job, and the number one answer is hiring quality people. Observe their behavior, and you will see little evidence of the seriousness of the task.

Many managers give lip service to the importance of hiring, and then go into an interview and wing it. Others complain about the time commitment and delegate the task. However, great managers work at the hiring process. They realize that great leadership starts with having outstanding followers.

4

LISTENING: THE UNDERUTILIZED ART

LEAVING WORK

How many times do you leave work feeling down, unfulfilled, and unappreciated—wishing that someone would just listen to you? We all feel better when we are listened to. We all have a need to be heard, understood and respected.

It's important for you to be an effective listener. If you are more of an extrovert than introvert, this will be huge challenge, but it's a challenge you must meet. Work on becoming an effective listener, and fewer people will be leaving work feeling down and unappreciated.

NOTICEABLY ABSENT

Ask anyone to list the skills necessary to become an effective leader, and listening will make every list. Ask the same people to take that list and identify those skills that are most noticeably absent in the workplace, and listening again makes the list.

We all know listening is important, and like most relationship skills, it's a skill that requires attention and practice. Although listening is a powerful communication tool, it is not as prevalent in the workplace as talking is.

What gets in the way? Let's take a look at a couple of reasons why people have not become effective listeners.

First, you are constantly rewarded for talking. How else can you show off and look smart. In meetings you must speak up to be noticed. In a world that is dominated by extroverts, people who like to communicate their ideas verbally, it's the silent ones, the introverts, who are thought to be weak.

Second, leaders often have a strong need to control. As a leader, you are responsible for performance, and many leaders take this to mean that they tell their followers everything. This control factor can be a huge detriment to you. Remember, to gain control, you must give up some control.

Third, you don't care about the person or are not interested in the subject. You have to care and be interested or you will just fake listening. You may have been taught that by paraphrasing, summarizing and questioning, you can become a better listener. This is only true when you come from a position of caring and interest. Do you care about the person? Are you interested in the subject?

Fourth, listening leaves you vulnerable. Listening can get you into soft areas, such as shared feelings. As important as this is, it's not always comfortable to get into these areas, and most managers don't like to show vulnerability. But as more and more research comes out on Emotional Intelligence, we know that it is those vulnerable soft areas that lead to our success.

Fifth, it's a lot easier to tell people what to do. It's fast, and easy, but it's not always effective. Giving direction is important; it's the way you give direction that you have to be aware of. If you are always telling, telling, telling, while never taking the time to check in and hear what your associates are thinking, you will have a lot of frustrated associates on your team.

Sixth, listening can lead to discomfort. If you really listen, you will allow for disagreement and honest discussion. It is a lot more comfortable hearing things that you want to hear.

All six of these reasons reflect on a strong managerial need; that is, to look good and be a strong decision-maker. But all six will slow you in your attempt to become an effective leader, because looking good and being strong has nothing to do with meeting others' needs. Your associates will never feel great about their contributions, if they cannot communicate their needs to you. It's very understandable that your associates will feel frustrated when they feel they are not heard.

So listening is hard and worthwhile work, but you must be willing to look at yourself, identify where you listen well and where you fall short, and constantly work to improve your listening ability.

DRIFTING

Your mind is constantly filled with internal noise. All that information that you have accumulated over time wants to occupy shelf space on your conscious brain. Your mind is constantly drifting, and although this is natural and healthy, you must be aware of this fact if you are going to be a better listener.

Most people speak at a rate of 125-150 words per minute, but your brain takes in information at a rate of approximately 600-1200 words per minute. That would leave a 400-1000-word gap, and that gap gives your brain a lot of time to focus on things other than just your spoken word. Since you can think so fast, and most talkers can't keep up, you go ahead and let your brain focus on the more interesting things floating around inside it. You stop paying attention and the speaker knows it.

Catch yourself when your mind goes off. Use your listening time to connect to what the speaker is saying, and because you have extra time to get the words, try to figure out what they are really saying.

Take this gap time to listen with empathy. Suspend judgment and attempt to identify where the other person is coming from and what their underlying feelings are. This will help you connect by filling your brain's gap time with some useful listening time.

YOUR INNER VOICE

Listen to yourself. What are you thinking, but not saying? Paying attention to your thoughts is a critical step to better listening.

Emotionally intelligent listeners are aware of how their endless thoughts can be a roadblock to what they intend to say. They also recognize that the inner thoughts of others hinder what they want to convey.

Others can sense it when your inner voice is taking over the conversation, and has stopped you from really listening to them. Your non-verbals will almost always give you away. You can't fake it. You must work with your inner voice if you want to be a great listener. Here are five tips:

1. Don't try to turn your inner voice off, it doesn't turn off. Understand that your mind will always be filled with noise, and that's okay. Taking time to understand how your judgments, perceptions and experiences are constantly playing in your mind will help you understand how they might be a barrier to better listening.

   Listen to yourself and be aware. You may find yourself judging, disagreeing, agreeing, defending, or denying. Know yourself. Know how your thinking may help or hinder your ability to listen. Very few people take the time to do this, and it is a critical key to effective listening.

2. Be aware of your tendency to rehearse. We often stop listening when our inner voice tells us we know the answer, and it starts helping us prepare for the next opportunity to break in with our brilliant insight.

   Catch yourself rehearsing. You will never gain full understanding of what the other person is saying when you are rehearsing. Try to connect and get underneath what the other is saying. Try to think about what is not being said.

   Don't assume you know where the other person is coming from. Use the listening encounter to learn something new. Stop rehearsing.

3. Focus on the purpose of the conversation. Work to understand. Ask questions, open-ended questions to learn more. Once you understand and you feel the need to persuade, do so. Listening is not silence. The best listening happens in real two-way conversations.

4. At times, disengage. When your emotions take over, there may be too much noise rattling around, and you may find you cannot listen at that time. It's okay to say:

"Mary, this is important, and I want to give it the time it deserves; let's set up a time when we can both give it the importance it deserves."

5. Acknowledge and summarize. Whenever you take the time to summarize, you show the other person you are listening. When you summarize correctly, you acknowledge that you really heard the message. If you summarize incorrectly, you give the speaker the opportunity to clear up any missed message. Either way, you win.

REALITY

The reality is that people need to feel wanted, worthwhile and important. When you take the time to listen, you are demonstrating that you care and respect the other person. And when you don't listen or fake it, how do you think the other person feels? It's probably the same feeling you get when you are ignored.

Never underestimate the power of listening. It is probably the greatest tool you can use to motivate people, and very few managers use listening to their advantage simply because they think that they have better things to do.

FRUSTRATION

Think about a time when you did a tremendous amount of work. You put in a great amount of time and sweat. You put together an excellent proposal that you were very proud of. And then you went in for a review of the proposal with your boss. And you probably left the meeting very frustrated. Why?

Most bosses think that the written word is meant to be critiqued, and it's because the written word is never complete enough. And most bosses get right into the judgment mode. They forget one main point: listen and understand first, and then judge and critique.

When you take the time to ask others to go through their idea with you before you get into working on the written word, you win big. Your associate feels great because he or she was listened to, you get a deeper understanding of what the true ideas are in the proposal, and you can give real value-added critique on how to improve the proposal.

Do you want to be a judge or a partner? Leaders are partners.

BE AWARE

There are plenty of barriers and filters that cloud our ability to listen. We all view the world in a different way, and we become vulnerable when we open up to someone else's viewpoint. Overcoming these barriers will help you to be viewed as someone special, someone who listens. Here are some thoughts on things you can do to become a more effective listener.

Don't interrupt. I know it's tough to be patient when you have "The Answer," so why wait? Well there are two main reasons to wait. First, someone might have a better answer than you do, so listen carefully and you might even hear it. Second, you will always have time to get your point in. If you constantly are known as an interrupter, you will frustrate others, shut them down and cut off communication.

Keep an open mind. It's important to know yourself, be aware of your listening weaknesses and be aware of when it is that you close off your mind to a particular subject or person. Admit your tendencies——Are you impatient? Are you the expert? Do you have a certain bias? Are you upset with the speaker?——and work on these tendencies whenever you find them getting in your way.

Listen for themes, not facts. If you need the facts, you can always go back and get them.

Ask questions, and really listen to the answers. Using effective probing skills is a great way to improve your listening. And remember, you don't need to know all the answers, but you do need people who will give you honest answers. Ask a lot of "why" and "why not" questions. Good people like it when you ask their opinion on things.

Get beyond the delivery. Not everyone is a great speaker; many have glaring flaws. Great listeners get beyond these flaws, and can pick up the content. This can be difficult, but keep at it; some of the best ideas come from poor speakers.

Stay calm. Don't overreact to emotionally charged or inappropriate words. If it bothers you, make a note of it, and make sure you talk to the speaker about it at the appropriate time.

Speaking of notes, get in the habit of keeping some. Experts have found that a listener remembers about 50% of what they heard immediately after the conversation ends and only 25% twenty-four hours later. By keeping simple notes, you can raise those percentages significantly.

Watch the non-verbals and the tone the speaker is using. Studies show that in one-on-one conversations, approximately 90% of the communication can come from those two sources, while only about 10% comes from the actual words.

Monitor your own non-verbals. Good listeners use active non-verbals when they are receiving a message. Do not be a stone face.

Take an inventory of your bad listening habits (daydreaming, overreacting, prejudging, time problems, interrupting, etc.). Overcome them and you will be amazed at what you will learn. Work on your bad habits every day; they will not leave you easily.

Take an inventory of the things in your office that distract you. Get rid of them, or at least have them out of sight or hand when you are listening to someone.

Don't fake listening by pretending that you are paying attention when all you are doing is rehearsing in your mind what you are going to say. Try really paying attention instead. Ask your team to tell you about your listening habits. Work to eliminate your bad listening habits.

Be curious. When you are curious you tend to explore things more. You listen more when you are in a curious mood. Try to be curious, you will be a better listener

Use your ears. There is a reason we have two ears and only one mouth, but do we ever overuse that one mouth. When we are doing all the yapping all we do is enjoy our own thoughts. When we are listening, we are likely to learn something. You never know where that next gem of knowledge will come from, so be listening for it.

5

MOTIVATION

Can you really motivate another person? Doesn't motivation come from within? Two great questions, questions that really make you think. Here's another one—Why is it that some people always get the most out of the people they work with, while others don't?

TRUST

Motivation always starts and ends with trust. But there is a tremendous trust gap in the workplace today. Management decisions such as downsizing and rightsizing have paid an awful toll on employee loyalty. More importantly, employees feel under appreciated because the boss shows a lack of sensitivity and lack of attention to their needs. The lack of effective caring leadership has left employees feeling put upon, used, and unsatisfied. There is a tremendous trust gap in business today, and it is demoralizing. The key themes of trust and loyalty are fading from the workplace.

Trust must return to the workplace, and it must start with you. It can happen, but don't think it's going to be easy. Building a trusting environment requires a long term commitment, and a watchful eye on what you are doing every day.

Let's talk about how you go about building and maintaining trust:

>   *First you've got to make this a priority in your daily life. Never let down.
>   *You must start by trusting others, only then can you expect others to reciprocate by trusting you.

*Never lie. Once you lose your integrity, you will never get it back.
*Be candid. Don't play games.
*Keep your promises.
*Admit it when you are wrong.
*Back your people up with others.
*Never talk behind a persons back.
*Don't pit one team member against another.
*Never criticize one team member when alone with another team member, just to make yourself feel good, or to justify something you are doing.
*Never hold a grudge.
*Never be manipulative; you will be found out.

As a leader, you will be held to very high standards. There are times when others take shots at you. Don't retaliate. If you are going to be held to high standards, you should strive to meet those standards.

STEP BACK

In order to motivate people, you need to give them adequate reasons to behave the way you want them to behave. Now this sounds easy, but it isn't, mainly because we basically expect people to act and think the way we do. We tend to assume that everyone gets our message when we tell them things, but often they don't. The reason this happens is that we have different behavior tendencies, different dreams, different perceptions and different values.

We have different filters that cloud the way we see things, but different is neither good nor bad, it's just different.

It's important to step back and recognize these differences and how your behavior may motivate or de-motivate others. Let's take a look at some of the more common styles.

1) The Bulldozer:

Bulldozers are power people. They like to be in control of situations. They need to influence others, and they do. Sometimes they are viewed very positively, but often they are viewed negatively because of their tendency to want to be in charge.

Bulldozers can be talented performers. They are often decisive, determined and results-oriented. At their best they are very efficient.

At their worst, bulldozers are impatient, fail to listen, are overbearing and over controlling. They will argue with you and fight you. They will readily take full credit for the success of any project they are involved in. They will tend to seek status.

Always treat the bulldozer, or anyone for that matter, with respect if you truly want to motivate him or her. Be strong, but don't bulldoze the bulldozer. You'll just lock horns and never come to a mutual satisfying agreement. Accept the fact that they will disagree with you more often than others. Whenever possible, give them recognition that is status related, they love to be in the limelight.

Never be subservient with bulldozers. They will take advantage of the weak leader.

Think a little about how you feel when you are being bulldozed. Now step back and ask yourself—Am I a Bulldozer?

2) The Social Director

Everyone likes the social directors. They are personable, outgoing and always positive. Their main concern is relationships. They hate conflict and take criticism personally, but you would never know it by their agreeable response to any criticism you may give. They readily accept any feedback you may give, almost too readily.

The social director needs to know you are supportive of him or her. They need you to accept them and you do this by paying attention to them. Be patient with the social director, explore avenues of conflict, and carefully avoid open confrontation. Show sincere interest in them, their ideas and especially in their feelings.

The social director fears rejection. Be careful not to use a bulldozing style with this person.

3) The Achiever:

Achievers get results. They are goal oriented people who are motivated by self-imposed standards of excellence. Sometimes they are team players, and sometimes they're not. Sometimes they are loners, and sometimes they aren't. Often they are experts in their field.

Achievers are not always consistent, and because of this they can be difficult to deal with. Like most people achievers need recognition, and they need it to reinforce that they are doing valuable and challenging work.

Achievers fears failure and are driven not to fail. They do not like to be dictated to, especially in areas where they have expertise. Get them involved in the decision-making process on how their projects should be accomplished.

4) The Team Player:

Team players are unselfish, candid and open. They are wonderful listeners, and are more than willing to share their own ideas. They are two-way communicators who want to hear other's ideas. They see the value in others contributions and are able to bring others into the team process.

Talented team players are rare and can be an invaluable resource to you. Never take them for granted. They often do things behind the scenes to make others look good. They don't tend to brag, and it is easy for you to overlook the real contribution this person is making. Be observant and recognize this person whenever you can.

The team player can be a challenge to you because they expect as much from you as you do from them. Be upfront and candid with the team player; ask them for advice. Get them involved in as many projects as possible; they will tell you if they have too much on their plate.

5) The Loner:

Loners are quiet, aloof and withdrawn. It's tough to get a good read on loners, they stay so much to themselves. Loners may just be shy, and are often excellent performers given the right situation. The loner could also be a passive aggressive type person and this type of person can hurt your team.

The loner avoids risk. You need to be patient in pulling things out of the loner, and you have to work hard in communicating with the loner because they will give you little feedback when you do communicate with them.

It's easy to ignore the loner, but don't. The loner usually has a need for security and if you ignore them, they will internalize the negative, and it will definitely affect their work.

These are just a few themes we can use when identifying the different types of people you will be working with. It is not my intention to put labels on people because that is not helpful. However, it is valuable to think about others and the way they are, to think about yourself and how you are perceived by others, and to put both thoughts together to determine how you can best communicate with and motivate others.

RECOGNITION

Do you ever get too much recognition? I would bet that you don't. I would also bet that you don't give too much to others. It is almost impossible to give a person too much recognition, as long as it is deserved.

Look for opportunities to applaud achievement, and then applaud it. Give credit to others for a job well done or for a useful idea, and do it often. Say thank you over and over.

Give a lot of specific positive feedback. People love to behave in ways that give them positive, immediate feedback, and they never get enough of it.

Respect the dignity and diversity of your associates. Learn about their ambitions, needs and dreams. Learn about their families and outside interests, and customize your recognition around what they value the most. It may be a small thing like sending a simple thank you gift to an associate's home, but it won't be a small thing when it arrives at the front door.

Celebrate often. Flowers, wine, balloons, pizza days, cider parties or just a champagne toast all do the trick. The celebration doesn't have to be fancy, and you can do one whenever you have a success story to tell. It's even great to celebrate when there is nothing to celebrate just to thank the team for their sustained hard work.

Hold bragging sessions. Encourage your associates to brag about their successes. And by all means brag about your team to others. Let others know how much you admire the people you work with. Never say a harsh word about your associates to others. Harsh words hurt.

When out of the office, place a call to an associate just to let him or her know you appreciate what they contribute. Always look for little ways you can let people know how much you appreciate their efforts and results.

DEFINING MOMENTS

We all have defining moments in our lives—new jobs, promotions, marriages, birthdays, accomplishments, having children, sickness, and even tragic events. You need to be with your associates when they are going through these moments.

Basically, you really need to care. Give your associates little gifts during the positive defining moments. Give them a smile and a pat on the back. And don't put it off—do it immediately.

Be there to listen during the tough times. Your associates may be going through some emotional trauma that you may feel uncomfortable dealing with, but just being there with them will really help.

People remember those who are with them during their defining moments. Being there is not only the right thing to do; it will help you in your on-going relationships with your associates.

Honor others and they will honor you.

FULFILLING WORK

General H. Norman Schwarzkopf put it well:

> "Meloy told Clemons that in his judgment, only four of the American's eleven battalion commanders were worth a damn, and that I was one of the four. I felt overwhelmed. I was surprised at how much the compliment meant to me—it made me reflect on how unhappy this Vietnam tour was compared to my first, during which I needed no praise because the work had been so fulfilling." [7]

Fulfilling work is motivational. There are millions of people driving to work each day with a pit in their stomach because their work is so boring and unimportant. You have the responsibility to find challenges for your associates, to get them to stretch and grow.

Let your associates know that their work is important, and tell them why you think that way. Help them to grow and do a little more each day. Don't let them flounder in a dull and boring job.

COMPENSATION

For work to be fulfilling, it must be accompanied by a fair compensation plan. Fair compensation programs may not be something that you can control, but they will affect who you can attract, and who you can retain.

Fair compensation will keep most people happy for a short period of time, but it is rarely a day to day motivator. Don't think of money as a long term motivator, it is the rare person who thinks he or she is paid too much.

The best compensation plans are the ones that tie directly into performance, such as a direct commission to a salesperson. But not all compensation is set up that way. At the very least, it is important to tie as much of the compensation into expectations, goals and results.

No matter what, you never have enough to compensate others as much as they would like. There are only so many resources a company has and those resources are always limited.

ISOLATION

Isolating a person from others is a cruel form of human punishment. And yet there are managers that practice this demoralizing and de-motivating custom as a matter of routine, and they don't even know it. If you fail to listen, if you fail to give deserved recognition, if you take credit for others work, or if you take your team for granted, you are guilty of the isolation sin.

People need attention, some more than others. Sam Walton knew the value of attention. He rode with his truck drivers, sat on his loading docks, listened to and even sang with his associates. He challenged, respected them and showed how much he cared by spending his valuable time with them. He also built a legendary business with them.

Take a look at how you are filling up your day. Who are you spending time with, and who is not getting any of your attention?

Paying attention to people is critical to your success.

USE AWARDS

Utilize any and all award systems available in your company. Whenever someone in your area deserves such an award, get it for them, and make it a big deal recognizing that they got the award.

Make sure that people on your team get all the titles they have earned. Get it for them immediately.

If your company has no award system, make one up. An example would be the Rose Award. Make up a plaque that has ROSE spelled out, with ROSE standing for Recognition Of Special Effort, and when someone does something special give them the plaque with a dozen roses. You are only limited by your creativity.

Pay attention, care and recognize over and over again.

6

VISIONS AND GOALS

"Some men see things as they are and say, why? I dream things that never were and say, why not?"

—George Bernard Shaw

VISION

Everyone in your group should know what you stand for, what you value, and what you expect. They must be aware of your definition of winning, and in what you believe your team can become. You must develop a clear vision of where you want the team to go, and then articulate it on a regular basis.

Establishing a vision is a wonderful way to show your team that you believe in them and in their future. A good vision takes into account both the realities of today and the possibilities of tomorrow. Your vision should be your dream of what the team can accomplish. It should be one that your team will feel proud of and, when it is reached, one they will brag about.

As you start to develop your vision, get some help. If you try to develop it on your own, you are limited to what you know and feel. When you include others, you bring more richness and breadth to the vision. Brainstorm with your team, talk to peers, bosses and customers, do some research on the Internet, and ask respected friends for their ideas. And before you write anything down, go back to your team one more time. After all, they are the most important part of the vision—the ones who will live and implement it.

Visions are highly customized, and so there are no rules or points that they must include, but here are a few words and ideas you might consider as you sit down to write the vision.

- Results to achieve
- Customers
- Quality Service
- Teamwork
- Importance of the individual
- Creativity and innovation
- Continuous improvement
- Competitive environment
- Respect and Trust
- Integrity

Work hard to include your team and get their buy-in. Encourage them to be critical and question the vision, and don't be afraid to change it. Revise it, and revise it and revise it again. A vision is not something that is developed over-night.

Once the vision is set, the work begins. The challenge and the real work is still ahead, and it's important to get the members of your team to see how they fit into the vision. Start by asking them to identify how their job fits in. Ask them about the barriers and obstacles that may hinder the vision. Ask them to define how your job fits in.

Once you get buy-in, it's important to sit down with each individual and talk about how their individual goals and team goals mesh together. Strong, clearly articulated goals are at the heart of vision attainment.

THE BIG D

How are you going to help your team achieve great things? Years of observing people mired in mediocrity may leave you wondering how you will be the one to make a difference. How you will help your team accomplish more than anyone thought possible.

You can make a difference, but only if your can get people excited and focused. The best way to do this is to get your team and each team member to do a little dreaming.

Growing up, we experienced new and exciting adventures every day. We dreamt about possibilities. We envisioned ourselves as a great entertainer, politician, sports hero or even a great firefighter. We could envision times of enthusiasm, excitement and fun.

We also learned very early that reality and our dreams did not always match up. Many reasons such as: physical shortcomings, lack of resources, negative feedback from peers and superiors, and a lack of dedication caused us to either fail at, or give up our dreams. And it hurt. We learned what failure was all about, and we learned to fear failure. Many learned to play it safe, and stopped dreaming. We still worked hard, it's just that we worked on someone else's dream, and what a shame.

It is important for you to get people to dream again. Get them to focus on what they want to accomplish with their life. Get them focused on the actions, behaviors, characteristics and even the pain it will take for them to go after their dream. When you see them getting a little excited about who they are, and what they can accomplish, you know you have reached them. You have taken a major step toward some solid goal setting.

Real goals start with dreams. They include a plan and a deadline. Great things happen when a person is working toward achieving a worthwhile goal. Passion, commitment, desire, and attitude are all attributes that one exhibits as they try to achieve such a worthwhile goal.

GOAL CLARITY

The time you spend with your team clarifying goals, focusing on both team and individual goals, will be invaluable. Expecting a lot from people, and getting them to buy into high expectations, is a critical management and leadership activity. Extraordinary behavior starts when people can visualize success and know that they can attain it.

Goals form the base from which all your training, coaching, appraising, motivating and even your organizational planning comes from. Without goals, what is it that your team will focus on and become committed to? When goals are clear, concise and agreed upon, your team members will have a mission they can strive to execute.

When goals are clear, challenging and worthwhile, people will want to work toward their achievement. A strong sense of urgency will replace boredom and complacency.

GOAL PREPARATION

You can't wing it when it comes to setting goals with your team. Goals must be well thought out. Planning and preparing for goal setting is a valuable use of your time. As you do your homework, the following questions should prove to be helpful:

For the team:

- What results does the team need to achieve?

- What are the team's strengths?

- What are the weaknesses?

For each individual:

- What are the person's strengths? Weaknesses?

- What does the person value?

- What goals would he/she see as a benefit?

- What will it take for the individual to attain the goal?

- Is the goal realistic?
- Does the individual have adequate control over the goal?
- Is the goal fair to the individual and the team?
- Is the goal challenging?
- How will the goal be measured?
- Is the goal clearly stated?

And as you are preparing for the goal setting session, so should each of your team members. They, too, should be considering a number of key questions:

- How has my performance been in the past?
- What can it look like if I have an extraordinary year?
- What do I do that is important for my success?
- What behaviors are keeping me back?
- Where do I want to be at the end of the year?
- Where will I be in three years?
- What obstacles will I need to overcome to reach my goals?
- What help (feedback, training, support) will I need?

After proper preparation both you and your individual team members will be more receptive to a solid goal setting session. But keep an open mind at this stage, because there are a number of reasons why you may choose to modify the goals.

GOAL MAGIC

You already know that there are no magic formulas that will satisfy every human encounter, but here are a few guidelines that should be helpful to the goal setting process.

- Be positive. Focus on what needs to be done and frame your goals in a positive manner. Nothing is worse than limiting or negative goals.

- Be specific. The more specific you can be about how the goal will be attained and measured, the better. But keep it simple and watch for ambiguity.

- Write goals down. Experts say you are three to four times more likely to reach your goals if you write them down. Ask each of your team members to write out their goals prior to the goal meeting. This will help set the stage for a solid two-way discussion.

- Support goals by a strong set of values. When people focus on goals they value, they are likely to work hard at achieving them. Be patient and flexible and keep an open mind about your people; you will have a better chance to set meaningful goals that match both the individuals values and the teams values.

- Agree on goals. Setting goals is a two-way street, and it requires a lot of time and effort. However, the time will be well spent in the long run.

- Have deadlines. A deadline gives life to a goal. A deadline will help each individual prioritize better.

- Upgrade goals. Circumstances rarely remain stagnant; things change all the time, and goals should be upgraded to reflect these changes. Reviewing goals on a regular basis is a valuable exercise.

- Set reasonable goals. Goals can be challenging, but people must believe they have a reasonable chance of reaching them before they put time and effort into their attainment.

- Measure goals. What gets measured gets focused on. Find ways to measure each goal.

OUTDO

Without mutual agreement, goals have little meaning. Time spent with each individual, clarifying goals, is some of the most important time you will spend.

A couple of years ago, Linda Eaton, a super talented training pro, and I came up with a simple model that can be used for the goal setting meeting. The model is called OUTDO, and it stands for the following:

O = Opening. How you should set the stage and open the meeting.

U = Understanding. Taking the time to understand the other person's point of view.

T = Talk. After getting the other's view, it is time to give your perspective.

D = Develop alternatives. If you encouraged real two way communication, you will likely have some disagreement. This is the time to discuss them.

O = Optimize the meeting. Summarize the meeting and agree on next steps.

This is a good model for any one-on-one meeting. Here is how it might work for your goal-setting meeting.

OPENING

- Be relaxed and open.
- Start the meeting by explaining its purpose, its structure and its benefits.
- Encourage the other person to be actively involved as a full partner in the discussion.

UNDERSTANDING

- Ask the other for his or her ideas on their goals.
- Review any forms or goal sheets they may have prepared.
- Listen and probe for clarification.
- Acknowledge what you've heard.

TALK

- Give your perspective.
- Add any pertinent data or information.
- Define areas of agreement or disagreement.

DEVELOP ALTERNATIVES

- Pinpoint where you stand on any disagreements.
- Problem solve together.

- Explore different ideas and solutions.

- Agree on an appropriate solution.

- Only as a last resort should you dictate a goal...

OPTIMIZE THE MEETING

- Summarize the discussion.

- Have the other person summarize the agreed upon goals.

- Put the goals in writing.

- Establish a follow-up feedback process that will keep the communication lines open.

When you complete the goal setting process, you have completed a major step in the cycle of management. The goals will form a foundation from which you can analyze performance, coach and counsel and eventually give a performance appraisal.

7

COACHING: A CRITICAL LEADERSHIP SKILL

GREAT COACHING DEFINED

Wouldn't it be great if you were given the opportunity to go out and choose five people from anyone who has ever lived to serve as your personal advisors? Who would you choose? Why do these people make your list? By answering those two questions you have just identified what you consider to be the keys to effective coaching, and if you can model the behaviors you think are critical to your advisors' success, you can become an effective coach.

By taking the time to identify what great coaching is to you will help you build a coaching style that is authentic. Being authentic, being yourself, is a fundamental coaching requirement.

IS COACHING NEEDED?

Jack Nicklaus is arguably the best golfer who ever lived. One of the reasons for Jack's success is his hunger to continually improve. Jack knows that practice, hard work and persistence are not enough. He knows that feedback from a trusted and knowledgeable observer will help him get better.

Well maybe Tiger Woods is the best golfer in the world, but you know what, he also spends a lot of time with his personal coach. He even rebuilt his awesome golf swing after winning the Masters championship by a record score.

If even the "best in the world" needs a good coach, think about the value that you can bring to your associates if you can master the art of coaching.

VISITING PRACTICE

Observe a successful sports team, one that has a long-term coach and a long-term winning record. You will find that in every case the coach will have a strong vision of success, an understanding of reality and a strong belief in his or her ability to get others to perform at a peak level. Observe further and you will find that the coach will spend time teaching, cajoling, motivating, encouraging and correcting. Observe his or her behavior as the coach:

> *Focuses on performance. A key to great coaching is to be able to identify and communicate to others the behaviors needed to be successful. The good coach emphasizes the good as much or more than the bad.

> *Is specific and descriptive. Everyone is clear about what is happening, and what needs to be done.

> *Gives immediate and constructive feedback. Timely feedback is given on a consistent basis.

> *Customizes feedback. Good coaches realize that people are at different levels of receptivity, and work to communicate in a way that each individual will understand.

> *Constantly returns to the fundamentals. He or she reinforces behaviors that lead to success. The coach will consistently look to raise the level of play by emphasizing the need to improve the fundamentals of the particular job or position.

PROWLING THE SIDELINE

We all can visualize the tough and menacing coach who stalks the sideline, ready to pounce on any small mistake. We expect that this coach will go on the attack and unload as soon as the offending player approaches the bench.

You may know of such a coach or, worse yet, played or worked for this type of person. And yet, as bad as this person might be, there is quite a bit we can learn from him or her.

Let's start with the good:

*This coach will give feedback in a timely manner.

*This coach will be very descriptive and specific about the observed performance.

But:

*This coach tends to criticize in public, embarrassing the offending performer.

*This coach tends to criticize the individual along with the performance, leaving the performer angry and defensive.

*This coach fears failure and tries to take control by yelling and screaming.

The menacing coach encourages change in behavior through the method of fear and intimidation. How do you feel when someone does this to you? This method of coaching is disruptive and should be avoided.

BELA KAROLYI

Bela Karolyi, the brilliant and controversial gymnastics coach, has taken in some magnificent Olympic moments, but very few will ever equal the legendary performance of his student, Kerri Strug. All Kerri did was become the dominant figure at the Atlanta Olympic Games by overcoming the pain of a badly sprained ankle, and vaulting the United States Women's Gymnastics team to its first ever Olympic Gold Medal.

Kerri's extraordinary performance was all about courage, dreams, commitment and resolve. When it became her time to go for it, she did, and moments later, she sank to the floor in obvious pain. Kerri was prepared to do well in the Olympics but more importantly, she was prepared to grab the gold when it was presented to her.

I don't know how Bela Karolyi stacks up as a role model for effective coaching, but I do know one thing he does with his successful athletes: he gets them to believe in him, and more importantly, in themselves.

Great coaches spend a lot of time getting people to believe in themselves, and this often leads to extraordinary results. Do you spend time helping people to believe in themselves?

THE BIG FIVE

There are five simple rules effective coaches live by. They are:

1. Observe the behavior. You will be a better coach if you can observe what is going on, rather than give feedback on second hand information.

2. Be specific and descriptive about the behavior you observed and about the desired behavior.

3. Focus on performance and behavior; never use personal attacks as a feedback strategy.

4. Be timely.

5. Praise in public and criticize in private.

THE GAG RULE

Great coaches are excellent observers; they are awake to what's going on around them. They also take advantage of anything that will give them an edge. One simple method that can give you an edge in giving feedback is something called the GAG Rule. GAG stands for:

> <u>G</u>et
> <u>A</u>cknowledge
> <u>G</u>ive

When coaching, try to <u>get</u> the other person's viewpoint first. Ask them questions about what he or she was trying to accomplish, and how they were going about the job. Ask them how they feel about their performance. By listening to the other person, you will gain information about the situation that you are not aware of, and as a result come up with solutions that have more depth. You also are gaining time to customize your solution to the particular individual you are coaching.

Next, <u>acknowledge</u> what you have heard. Most managers skip this critical step. Don't. This step will show the other person that you have listened to them and understand where they are coming from.

Finally, <u>give</u> your ideas. Now that you understand the situation fully, you are ready to offer solutions that are more likely to be accepted and acted upon.

COACHING MISTAKES

We all make mistakes, but luckily we grow if we can learn from them. Answer the following questions, and consider if there is anything holding back your coaching ability.

*Do you assume too much, and jump in without knowing or observing what is going on?

*Do you do more telling than listening when giving feedback?

*Do you coach only when you see mistakes? Only when you see the good things?

*Are you threatening?

*Are you negative?

*Do you skirt issues?

*Do you focus on personalities rather than skills?

*Do you avoid tough situations?

*Do you say: "Here is the only way to do this; it's the way I do it?"

*Do you take your time coaching, or are you always in a rush?

*Do you treat everyone exactly the same?

Coaching is tough work. Try to avoid mistakes that limit your effectiveness.

OUTDO MODEL

Coaching can happen at any time and just about anywhere. It can be a quick two-minute encounter in the hall or a formal meeting in your office. If you are going to hold a formal meeting, consider using the <u>OUTDO</u> model as a format. To review, OUTDO stands for:

* <u>O</u>pening the session
* <u>U</u>nderstand the others viewpoint
* <u>T</u>alk (give your view)
* <u>D</u>evelop alternatives
* <u>O</u>ptimize the meeting

Prior to the session:

*Review all relevant materials—data, records, notes, etc.
*Identify both strengths and weaknesses, ask:
  - What is this person doing right—be specific
  - What is this person doing wrong—be specific
  - Is this important?
  - How will I help this person get better?
  - What do I want to accomplish as a result of this meeting?
*Commit to being a good listener during the meeting.

<u>O</u>pening the session

*Clearly state the purpose and format of the meeting.
*Identify the benefits to the other person
*Encourage the other person to be an active participant in what you expect to be a two-way conversation.

<u>U</u>nderstand the other person's view:

*Ask a lot of open-ended questions.
*Listen.
*Don't interrupt, be patient.
*Acknowledge what you have heard.
*Probe to see how receptive the other person is at this time.

Talk:

    *Give your views.

    *State where you agree and disagree.

    *Give some specific improvement ideas (if improvement is the reason for the coaching session).

    *Probe for receptivity.

Develop alternatives:

    *Examine the different approaches and solutions available.

    *Build on any ideas that come up, but are not totally thought out.

    *Identify any consequences or rewards.

    *Be aware that easy agreement might not be real agreement.

    *Choose the best alternative.

Optimize the meeting:

    *Get the other person to summarize the plan.

    *Be specific as to follow-up. Who, what, where, when, why, and how.

The OUTDO meeting is not the final piece of feedback; it is just one piece of feedback. It does set the stage for further formal and informal coaching sessions.

TECHNIQUE

Just a quick word on technique. Management models are terrific, but only if they are genuine. If you are using models to help you to manipulate people, the model will eventually hurt you. But if you are using the model because it helps give you a structure, and keeps you focused on helping the other person, you will succeed.

COACHING QUICKIES

Here are fifteen thoughts that may help you to be a better coach:

1. Listen and observe. These critical skills take concentrated effort and hard work.

2. Be very clear and open about what you want to have your team accomplish. Challenge your group to become extraordinary.

3. Give feedback often, and always tie the feedback to the results you envision for your group.

4. Communicate with clarity and with concern for others. Keep communication lines open.

5. Be yourself. Never be phony.

6. Give credit to others.

7. Never hold grudges.

8. Be an optimistic role model.

9. Let your team members know where they stand with you, never leave them guessing. This is not always easy in the messy environment we are in today, but clarity is always important. Work to clarify things.

10. Believe in your people and make sure they know it.

11. Demand continuous improvement from your team, and place that same demand on yourself.

12. Keep disagreements private, and never hesitate to praise others in public.

13. Follow through.

14. Be available, be persistent, be decisive, and be consistent.

15. Believe in yourself and in your ability to make a difference in people's lives.

ACCEPTING FEEDBACK

We all need feedback in order to learn and grow, but it's not easy to accept the feedback we get. When it is negative, we tend to clam up or get defensive when we need to listen for the grain of truth that is almost always present. And the positive is usually superficial, and we fail to get any real depth of satisfaction from it.

Knowing that these tendencies are present often discourages people from giving feedback to others. Don't do that. People need your feedback, and only the top managers, leaders and coaches have the courage and compassion to give this needed feedback to those they care about.

8

DEVELOPING OTHERS

THE LEARNING ENVIRONMENT

Are you committed to learning? Are you building a work environment that supports learning? Everyone gives lip service to building a learning organization, but few organizations go beyond lip service.

Real learning takes place on the job. Observe your work environment to make sure that your team has interesting challenges that they can learn from. Observing team members on the job and giving them solid feedback is the key to real learning. If you are not involved by giving solid and on-going feedback, you don't have a learning environment.

Formal training can be an effective supplement to what your team learns on the job, but it is never a substitute for what people learn from their day to day experiences.

Your involvement is the key in setting an environment of learning. Take the time to set learning goals for team members, and for yourself. Being a positive learner yourself will help set the stage for others wanting to learn.

The time you spend developing others is invaluable. You may even find yourself learning more than they do.

THE DEVELOPMENT MEETING

Very few people sit down with their manager to talk about their development, and this is a shame. Having a talk with team members about their development is one of the most important things you can do. It is one of the ways you show that you really care about them as people and not as just employees.

Each year sit down with every member of your team, and have a discussion about his or her development. If your group is too big, make sure that you are meeting with the key people, and someone else is doing a developmental review with the rest.

When you meet, you will want to emphasize how much you think of them and that you would like to help them as they strive to grow as a worker and as a person. Tell them that this is the type of meeting where you want to focus on how they are doing as they work to attain their dreams and goals.

Prior to the meeting it's important for you to think about each person, his or her progress, and his or her developmental needs. Make an assessment as to where each person stands, and where you see them going. Solicit feedback from others. Ask them to identify learning needs they think would be valuable for individuals who report to you.

During the meeting, develop a plan and come to an agreement on one or two key developmental needs. Work with the associate to customize a plan to meet his or her individual needs, and assure the associate that you want to partner with them to help them accomplish their plan.

In conducting the meeting it's important to:

- Explore the team member's experiences
- Talk about their dreams and goals
- Identify future challenges and changes
- Focus on specific needs
- Create a development plan

Your meeting is basically a conversation between two respected professionals, so make sure your associate gets a chance to talk. Listen carefully, and give your view as to his or her development needs. Finally, reach an agreement on appropriate activities to meet those needs.

RECEPTIVITY

One of the most overlooked parts of the learning process is the receptivity of the learner. It's relatively easy to get a high level of receptivity from new hires who are eager to learn, but the old timers are a real challenge.

To raise receptivity in others, start by taking a hard look at yourself. If you never attend any training or put training down, don't expect your team to be thrilled when you tell them they are enrolled in a three-day training program next month. Make sure that you are positive about the training programs or learning opportunities you get to attend. Bring back some new ideas and share them with your team as soon as you return from the learning experience.

People go through a number of different stages of receptivity before they become active learners. Here are three common stages.

- Initial enthusiasm: You sell the training to a team member and you get a positive response.

- Doubting: As the time approaches to go to the training, the team member starts doubting whether time away from the job is worthwhile. Realize that this stage will occur, and you may need to re-sell the person on the benefits of the training.

- Scheduling: Make sure the date is clear early. Plan on helping the associate with conflicts that come up that would force him or her to cancel the training.

Not everyone needs or wants formal training. There are so many learning opportunities that they could benefit from, such as visiting another office or working on a community project, and it is important that you work to customize a plan with each individual. And even when you work hard to customize the learning opportunity, don't be surprised if you get some reluctant behavior from the associate. Remain positive, even in the face of reasonable objections.

When a team member returns from a training program, schedule some time to sit down and discuss what was learned. If it would benefit the entire team to hear the ideas, schedule some time for the team to get together. By showing genuine interest in what was learned, you will automatically raise receptivity.

DIFFERENCES

It would be great if everyone learned in the same way and at the same speed, but that's just not the way it is. There are so many different ways that people prefer to learn. Here are a few:

- Some learners are very people oriented and learn best from others. Giving them a lot of analysis and logic may not be the most effective way for them to learn. They don't want a lot of lecture.

- Some people are very security minded. They love lecture, but hate outdoor adventure training.

- Some people are great problem solvers and would learn a lot from case studies, but would not gravitate toward a lot of open ended discussion

- Most people learn from doing; others learn by thinking. A combination of the two really raises self-awareness.

- Some like ideas, rather than feelings, to understand different problems.

- Some are practical and logical, while others love the abstract.

- Some like hands on experience, while others prefer brainstorming sessions.

It's not easy to identify learning experiences that work for everyone, so don't try. Do try to offer varied training opportunities so that different learners all have a better chance of picking up the knowledge, skill or behavior they need to learn. When in doubt it's generally a good rule to get adults involved actively in the learning process.

Try to put variety in your training. Don't be afraid to be creative.

THE LEARNING CIRCLE

As you consider any learning opportunity, it would be valuable to consider the different stages a learner goes through.

- Question: The learner understands that there is a skill that needs more development.

- Thinking: The learner thinks more about needed development and makes a decision on what to do about it. Often the learner will do nothing and no learning takes place.

- Receptivity: The learner decides to pursue the skill and looks for ways to develop it.

- Testing: The learner takes new ideas and tries them out. If they get accurate feedback at this stage, they are more likely to incorporate the learning into their routine.

- Reflecting: This is an important and overlooked stage. Adults learn best from each other, and they really learn when they are able to reflect on how they are working on real problems and opportunities.

As adults go through the stages, they learn and grow. It's important for you to think about these stages when you are working on learning opportunities for your group.

KEY

Never stop giving feedback on the job, especially when someone has done something extremely well or to someone who has just failed. Reinforcing great behavior is terrific, but just as terrific is learning from failure. Never hesitate to give solid behavioral feedback and coaching. Adults learn best when they receive accurate feedback.

9

APPRAISING OTHERS

HERE IT COMES AGAIN

At the end of every year comes time for the performance appraisal; a look back on the accomplishments for the year. It is the final step in the management cycle that started with the initial goal setting session you held early in the year with your direct reports. A lot happens during the year, and it is critical for you to capture the true flavor of what really happened, and communicate the results back to each member of your group.

PREPARATION

Be prepared. This certainly is a key theme, and as busy as you are, you must find time to think and prepare for each person you are going to review. So much of what you do is spur of the moment, that there is little time to prepare, but with performance appraisals you must take the time.

Start by reviewing the goals you set early in the year and review any revisions that were made to these goals during the year. Gather specific evidence of performance, such as: results achieved, obstacles overcome, coaching notes you may have made, correspondence from others and any other relevant information. Look at the information as objectively as you can. Compare the results against agreed upon measurement standards as much as you can.

Not everything can be measured, and it's important that a well thought out subjective perspective be added to your assessment. Think about barriers that may have been deterrents to the results, and fairly evaluate those factors. Add in the intangibles, extras that the person brings to the table, and think about any circumstances that may have led to a lower or higher level of performance.

Outline all the points, good and bad to be covered in the review. Determine a fair rating, and set up a time and place for the review to take place.

Give each member of your group a copy of the form you will use for the evaluation. Ask them to review it and to come in prepared to talk about their performance for the year.

Fill out the appropriate form. Think carefully about the wording in the narrative since this ordinarily becomes part of the permanent record of each team member.

RECENCY AND HALO

You are only human, and it's easy to let your own bias slip in during the evaluation. Be careful, you have to be fair with everyone.

Be aware of the "Halo Effect." This happens when either exceptional work or poor work in a specific area overshadows the entire body of work done during the year. Exceptional and poor work are both important considerations in a performance appraisal, but you must look at all the work an individual contributes during the year if you are to give a fair appraisal.

Also, be aware of the "Recency Effect." This is when recent events overshadow the year-long effort. This is an easy trap to fall into.

A performance review must include the whole year and total performance. Be fair and complete.

NO SURPRISES

When you appraise a person's performance they should not be surprised by anything they hear in the appraisal. If you have done your job and coached and given effective feedback throughout the year, each member of your team will know exactly where they stand, and know what they should expect in the performance review.

Surprises come when communication and feedback are lacking during the year. Employee surveys constantly point out that people are not getting feedback during the year and never receive an appraisal at the end of the year. This is inexcusable and it is poor management.

Make feedback a priority. Do it throughout the year, and do it with everyone who reports to you. There should be no surprises at an appraisal meeting. As a matter of fact, very little should be said at the meeting that wasn't said during the year.

THE MEETING

An appraisal is an important feedback tool. Anytime you sit with someone to talk about him or her, take it very seriously. Here are some ideas that should help you run the meeting in an effective manner.

- Open the meeting by clarifying the purpose of the meeting. Give a brief overview of the structure you would like to follow.

- Start by asking the team member to review how he or she thought the year went.

- Listen and ask questions, especially if you are getting some surprises.

- Next, present your evaluation, and the rationale behind it. Tell your associate where you agree with his or her own evaluation, and explain any reasons where you might disagree. Be sure to praise good performance, and keep thoughts on poor performance specific and concise.

- Give your overall rating. Explain how you came up with it. Keep to the facts.

- To conclude the meeting, make a transition and start talking about the future. If appropriate, start talking about the goals and challenges for the upcoming year. End on a positive note.

ANXIETY

Sometimes review meetings can cause a little anxiety for you and your associate. After all, you are rating the associate for an entire year, and putting the rating into a permanent record. While most reviews go well, here are three responses you should be prepared to handle.

- Disagreement with the rating. When this happens, listen and ask questions. Go back to the evidence for your rating and ask questions around that. If you find reasons to change the rating, do so. You are not infallible.

- Emotional, angry response. Remain calm and patient let the associate vent. Listen and question them, but don't give in. If the anger gets personal, stop the meeting and allow for a cool down stage, but never allow disrespect. During the cooling off time, think about why the associate is reacting with anger, and ask yourself if there is any truth in what is being said.

- "Didn't think I was being rated in a certain area." This should be a rare statement if you do a good job of goal setting. Go back to your goal discussion and make sure it was clear as to the expectations for the year. It could be that you did not do a good job of goal setting.

REVIEW YOURSELF

Prior to and after the review, you should think about these nine questions. Your handling of the appraisal is critical, and your team members will judge you harshly if you handle it poorly.

- How well did you structure the discussion?

- How well did you explain the criteria for the rating?

- How well did you explain the specific performance and behavior that made up the rating?

- How well did you listen?

- How much of the discussion was two-way?

- How well did you do in asking relevant questions?

- How well was the summary handled?

- How well was the closing handled?

- How can you improve on the meeting?

10

TEAMWORK

The subject of teams is one of the most popular subjects in business today. And the word "team" is used to describe just about any group that works together. But real teams are more than groups of people, and real teamwork is hard to find.

A PERSONAL STORY

Please forgive me as I relate a personal story. It's a story about the 1981 Seton Hall Prep Wrestling Team, a team I had the privilege of coaching. And it's a fond memory of what it takes to be a successful team.

STATE CHAMPS

I was in my final year as a high school teacher and coach. I was coaching a talented group of wrestlers, a team that had an excellent mix of experienced hard working achievers, and high potential young inexperienced wrestlers. After a slow start, this group ended up winning the group state championship.

I wish I could tell you that I knew what I was doing as far as leading this team, but nothing could be further from the truth. I coached out of instinct and just tried to do what was right. A lot of luck seems to follow when you do what's right. Here are ten lessons I learned from the team.

1. Go for the gold. We talked about winning and the commitment it takes to win. We talked about it everyday. We talked about hitting our peak right at tournament time. We talked about the fun, the hard

work and the need for everyone to help out. Our goals were high, we expected a lot from each other.

2.   Believe in the team. Early in the season, we had a couple of tough defeats. After winning a Christmas tournament, we lost two of our first three dual meets. Our next match was against one of the perennial state powers, a match we were not expected to win. Two days before the match, following a tough but good practice, I gathered the team together. I told them in a slow and deliberate manner that no matter what happened; I would never stop believing in them. And I meant it.

At our banquet at the end of the year, one of the captains said that short speech was the turning point in the season. They knew I meant every simple word. We won the match and went undefeated the rest of the way.

3.   Ask others to share in the leadership role. My assistant coach was captain of his college team and a state champion in high school. He was also a terrific person. We agreed early on that we would be co-coaches and would be responsible for unique parts of the program. There is no rule that says there has to be only one leader.

4.   Build a leadership core within the team. We were unique in that we had five captains, and we gave them a lot of responsibility. They got involved in team decisions, team problems and team celebrations. They handled themselves with great maturity and took a great deal of pride in their role.

5.   Don't be an expert in everything. I was lucky to have a lot of good people around to help out, so I made sure they had a lot to do. My assistant handled most of the teaching. He was much better at it than I was. The captains also taught and were responsible for weekend or holiday practices. I was there all the time, but they were in charge.

6.   Don't be totally inward focused. We often had Alumni come back to visit us. Many were college wrestlers and we never missed the chance to have them teach the team the new techniques they were learning and using at their level.

7.   Ask for the effort. If you want the team to succeed, individuals on the team must give a total effort to reach team goals. You need to work

with each individual to identify what drives and motivates them, and then emphasize these things with them often. When you get people focused on their dreams and identify how being on the team helps them, you can ask them to contribute to the teams effort.

8. Trust them. Early in the year we decided that everyone on the team could take four days off from practice with no questions asked. Now this didn't include time off for sickness or other legitimate excuses. Only two wrestlers out of 53 ever took advantage of this. Trust them and they will repay your trust.

9. Be with them, not above them. As the coach, I had to be in the hot practice room observing, motivating, teaching, correcting and praising. My responsibility was to be with the team, not off in some nice Coach's Room reading press clippings.

10. Thank them. Thanking people for a great effort never gets old. Never tire of thanking and praising others, and do it in front of the rest of the team.

These ten ideas are good ones to think about as you work with your teams. Let's take a look at some other ideas.

CARL LARSON

Successful teams identify their purpose and goals early and often. They regularly discuss the resolve and commitment that will be necessary for them to attain the high standards they set for themselves. Research on teams has one common theme and that is goal clarity. In his book <u>Teamwork</u>, noted teamwork expert, Carl Larson, puts it well:

> "Two insights about teams emerged early, consistently, and very emphatically from our interviews. First, high performance teams have both a clear understanding of the goal to be achieved and a belief that the goal embodies a worthwhile or important result." [8]

Carl emphasizes that having a clear, elevating goal was present in every successful team he had studied, and is missing in every unsuccessful team.

You really need to spend a lot of time discussing what is worthwhile and what is important to your team, and then setting goals consistent with that discussion. Get the team to agree on bringing the goal to life by painting a picture of what will be accomplished by attaining it. Be innovative, look for new alternatives and ideas, and make sure the final goal is challenging and achievable.

Focus on the team goals regularly. Work with others on the team to keep it current. Work to clarify them whenever they gets fuzzy. Once you have goal clarity—go for it.

OPENNESS

Trust is critical to any team's success. You won't have real teamwork if trust is breaking down. Where there is little or no trust, you may see a group of people working together, but there is little chance they are working as a team. And there is little chance that you will witness the increased productivity that a real teamwork can bring to the table.

Trust starts with the team being open and being willing to communicate with each other. To foster trust, deal with conflicts immediately. Listen, observe and always be willing to jump in when you see that communication is breaking down.

Be on the watch for the team member with the personal agenda. It's important for all team members to be on the same page going after the same goal. Hidden agendas, such as personal political gain, are destructive to team development.

Integrity is always important. Any breach in integrity will always lower the trust level.

If you see the team floundering, be ready to intervene. Make sure that you have set up an environment where team members can admit mistakes and show vulnerability. Teamwork has little to do with perfection. Mistakes happen and are often the fault of an individual team member. Allow for mistakes and use them as great learning opportunities for the team.

Listen and observe a lot. Be as much a learner as you are a contributor. Only if you are open, will the team be open to you. Only when you trust, will the team trust you.

FAILED TEAMWORK

There are a lot of reasons why a team may fail. Three seem to stand out: poor leadership, poor goals and poor communication.

When the team leader is arrogant, insensitive, non-supportive, or overemotional, there is little chance that there is any real leadership being exhibited. This type of "leader" is usually bulldozing ideas because they fear losing control. Or they are totally aloof because they are afraid to make a decision that would be unpopular with senior management. Either way this "leader" is ineffective and is not going to be able to build an extraordinary group working synergistically.

Teams that are confused about their purpose will usually fail. Poor teams either lack real goals, lack goal clarity, or lack goals that are worthwhile. As a result, there is little the team members can commit to. They may even be confused as to why they need a team to accomplish the tasks in front of them.

Poor teams are noted by a lack of communication. Sharing ideas, listening with respect, and being candid with each other are present on good teams, and noticeably absent on weak teams. The poor communication leads to tension and conflict, guarded conversation, limited involvement and poor results.

You must be aware of these three issues and insure that they don't creep into your team or group. Be aware; these issues come up all the time.

TEAM LEADERSHIP

Leadership can come from any member of the team. The appointed leader is not always the real team leader. There can often be more than one team leader, and team leadership will evolve as the team process evolves.

To be a real team leader, you must truly care about the team and its goal. You also need to be able to let go and let others on the team take the lead in areas they have real expertise.

You can be more effective as a leader only when you are consistent in your behavior and always striving for outstanding results that support the team's worthwhile goal. Get the team to focus on what can be done. Get them to question and challenge "why" and "what" is being done.

To lead you must be sensitive to the needs and dreams of others, as well as your own needs and dreams. But mainly you need to get outside of yourself and focus on others. Be supportive, but be demanding. Be open and work to observe and listen. And by all means, show some vulnerability. You don't always have to be right.

GREAT TEAMS

As companies get leaner, the greater the need for teamwork. There is a great need to share ideas and information. Goal clarity, high expectations, flexibility, trust and collaboration will be needed as internal competition starts to fade away.

Great teams focus on results. They get better results than an individual can. They make sure that all the members of the team are able to share in the attainment of those results.

Great teams solve problems and look at alternatives before taking action. They openly share and discuss opposing ideas. They combine solid evidence with excellent intuition to make decisions.

Trusted team members lead great teams. There are often a couple of people who lead the team effort. Team members have faith in each other.

Great teams often have conflicts, but deal with it in a positive and timely manner. They deal with multiple goals and handle contradictions well.

Great teams are flexible, resilient and deal with change in a positive manner.

COMPENSATION

One of your greatest challenges will be on effectively managing team compensation issues. When real teamwork results in outstanding results, team members will, and should, feel that they each made significant contributions. Each individual will feel that the team could not have accomplished what it did without their participation.

As a leader you must balance the feelings that the individuals each have with the actual contributions they made to the team. Quite frankly, not all team members are equal; some are much more valuable than others. Your challenge is how to compensate each team member fairly.

It is best to identify the compensation issues as the team is being developed. You may have little choice if you are tied into some company policy, or you may have total freedom to come up with a creative plan. But never take compensation planning lightly.

If possible get the key parties together as the team is being formed. Put all the issues out on the table, roll up your sleeves, and get prepared for some hard and frank discussions. And when all is said and done, it will still be up to you to make the right decision. Always keep in mind that the way you handle compensation issues will be scrutinized, and will affect how team members view you as a leader.

Never take compensation issues for granted. They are rarely easy. There are few rules, and even fewer helpful hints, on how to come up with an effective plan, but it is up to you to come up with one.

FORMATION STEPS

As you help new teams form think about the following 10 steps. Most teams go through these before they become a real team.

1. The Dream. Teams form because individuals have a dream that things will be better if a team, rather than individuals were working in a particular area. Dreaming is an important part of team formation. You need to be able to visualize how things will be better well before the team is formed.

2. Pre-formation Meetings. Spending a lot of time up front with perspective team members is crucial to team success. You should share ideas with the perspective members on the work that has to be done, and follow up with how an ideal team relationship would really work. Clear up as many of the questions on what team success would look

like. Also spend some time on the negatives the team may face going forward.

3. Vision/Purpose. All successful teams have a clear and understandable vision. Spend time with team members working on developing this vision. This will be crucial to the teams' long term success.

4. The Business Plan. Putting "who, what, where, why, how, and when" down in writing is critical. Make sure that roles and responsibilities, critical measurements, deadlines and objectives are included in the plan.

5. The Dating Period. This is the time right after the initial formation. This is the time when you find out whether the team will work as planned. Don't be fooled by early team success, because it's during this time that the team is on their collective "best behavior." It's a time when problems are either ignored and will blow up later, or they are blown out of proportion now. Don't let your guard down during this important time. Your coaching and guidance are very important during this early stage.

6. Formation. It's only after the five stages above that a team is really formed. And even then there is still more to be done.

7. Resistance. There will come a time, early where the team will become a little dysfunctional. There will be some infighting and some inward and outward resistance to whether the team is going to work. Be aware of this stage. Your coaching and mentoring is critical here. Teams break up if this resistance is not addressed

8. Communication. Real communication happens after the team has worked with each other for a period of time. No matter what the preparation was that the team went through before forming, they will not be great at communicating until they have spent time with each other.

9. Conflict/Concerns. Just as you think the team is on its way, conflict gets in the way. Conflict can and will happen. It happens to all good teams. These conflicts can get out of hand and put the workings of the team in jeopardy.

10. Performance. Teams whose members really care about each other can get to real performance, and this is where you see real productivity take place. But teams rarely get to this level without going through many or all of the previous nine steps. Be aware of these steps and you can help your teams become successful and thrive.

Your active involvement with your teams never ends. Working with them can be difficult, because your dealing with a combination of individual egos with varying emotions—trying to get them to collaboratively work together as one—wow that isn't easy. More importantly working with teams can be extremely rewarding, especially when you see the impressive productivity gains that will result.

11

CONFLICT

HUMAN NATURE

As ranking members of the animal kingdom, a system that is predicated on surviving conflict, we humans have become quite sophisticated when it comes to building conflict into our daily lives. We can take the most trivial of circumstances and make it a major problem. When it comes to drumming up conflict, we are most creative.

It's a wonder why we, the highly evolved human, can't seem to find a way to eliminate, or at least minimize, conflict from our daily lives. Why is it that conflict is so prevalent? Let's take a look at a few key reasons:

- Differences. We are all different. We have different values, backgrounds, preferences, thoughts, behaviors and blind spots. None of us see things exactly as another person sees them.

- Control. Humans are the most control oriented of all the animals. We want to control everything, but as our lives and living environment gets more complex, it becomes more difficult for us to gain and maintain control. When our expectations are disrupted, as they often are in this messy world we live in, our feeling of being in control is minimized. The reactions of uncertainty, denial, anger, frustration and rationalization that are a result of our lack of control can all lead to conflict.

- Inner Dialogue. We fear many things, and our fears cloud our thinking by allowing negative thoughts to dominate our inner dialogue. Our thoughts are often filled with worry and judgment, and they cloud what is really happening. Negative thoughts can be very powerful, and eventually they lead to conflict.

- <u>Fear of failure</u>. It's still not popular for managers to encourage failure, despite all the literature that supports failure as a key learning experience. As a matter of fact, failure is still something to be avoided. C.Y.A. memos, politics, internal competition all are a result of our fear of failure, and all are conflicts waiting to happen.

PERSPECTIVES

Because no two people are alike, and because every situation is different for each individual, conflicts are inevitable. Conflicts can come up anytime people get together, even when the individuals involved like and respect each other.

You may have members of your team who are charismatic, creative, inspiring and engaging, people who are willing to push the limits. You will have other team members who are careful, traditional and shy, people who are slow to change. Some of your team may be practical and cost conscious, while others want to try new things no matter what they cost. Some may be great at talking through ideas, while others like to listen and think ideas through.

Because we are complex and different, conflict will happen. Here are a few circumstances that happen every day:

- Joe things Mary jumps too quickly and makes too many snap decisions, while Mary thinks Joe takes forever to make up his mind.

- Sara thinks that Bob talks too much and never listens, and Bob thinks Sara is aloof and never participates in the key decisions.

- Gary thinks Gene is overly concerned with detail, while Gene things Gary is off the deep end with his abstract unfocused thinking.

- Judy thinks that Ann provides too many options, while Ann thinks Judy lacks imagination and creativity.

- Marie thinks Rudy is overpowering, while Rudy thinks Marie is too cautious.

These people are looking at the same situation through different lenses. They may be all great workers; they just have different frames of reference. It's up to you as the leader to recognize these differences, talk to your team members about the different ways people see things and react to them. Talk to the team about the reality that people will differ in their thoughts and approaches. Talk to them about the value that can come by having diversity in behaviors and preferences. It sure would be boring if everyone thought alike.

Be proactive and discuss differences regularly with your team. Be observant and point out specific ways that the team benefited by the differing perspectives. Never avoid the fact that we are all diverse and different. Maximize it by pointing out the benefits and power that diversity brings to the table.

Be a student of diversity. There is a tremendous amount of research available on how men and women behave in different ways. But always be careful that you don't use generalizations when it comes to behavior. It is difficult to categorize human behavior.

NEGATIVITY COORDINATORS

While understanding and encouraging different views and preferences is good, never allow a negativity coordinator to be part of your team.

A negativity coordinator is a person who is very vocal about how bad everything and everyone is at work.

- "Compensation is bad."
- "People are unappreciative"
- "The boss plays favorites"
- "The people who do all the work never get the credit"
- "Senior management is dumb"
- "Nobody cares"
- "Most of our work is stupid"
- "Nobody ever gets us the things we need."

These are the words of the negativity coordinator, and they are disruptive and dangerous.

If the negativity coordinator was always miserable, others would quickly dismiss him or her. After all, who would want to be around such a person on a regular basis? But the negativity coordinator is often charming, and is often an expert at framing things to get others to think the same way that they do. They are great at sensing when the time is right to complain and gripe, and they often do it with a smile on their face.

The more likeable the negativity coordinator is the more dangerous. They feed on people in small groups and one-on-one. They work hard to get others to reinforce their point of view.

The coordinator believes in what they say, but lacks the courage to be open with you. They value job security and wish that others would speak out to get the changes they want. As a result, they are supportive when you are around, but are assassins behind your back.

You have to be awake and aware to catch a negativity coordinator. Look for a change in an individuals performance or behavior. Watch for one-on-one closed-door meetings that never took place before. Watch for the immediate cutting off of conversation whenever you come on the scene. Watch out for patronizing behavior to your face, but silence and no support at meetings.

When you are sure that it is negativity behavior that you are observing, deal with it promptly. Let the negativity coordinator know that you will not tolerate such behavior. Ask them why they are negative, why they are unhappy. Look for the grain of truth in what they say, and pledge to change things that appropriately need to be changed. Make the coordinator know how you feel about their behavior and how it disrupts the team. And ask the person to change.

If the negativity coordinator does not change, it is best you work with them to find another job. Even a superstar can poison a team.

BILL PARCELLS

A couple of years ago I was watching television and heard what I believe is a critical theme when it comes to conflict. It came from the outstanding NFL coach, Bill Parcells. What I heard him say was:

> "When I was young, I would fight every battle. I was like Don Quixote fighting windmills. Now I will still fight battles, but only if I feel it is important."

There are times when you need to intervene and handle conflict, but there are other times when all you are doing is interfering. Your judgment is critical as to when to intervene. Pinpointing problems and investigating solutions is part of your responsibility. Getting involved in every conflict is not.

When you do intervene, be prepared to probe and listen. Don't jump to any early conclusions. It's easy to get to a bottom line, don't.

If the conflict has gotten to where people are angry with each other, you are the one who has to be the calming influence. Try to get the angry parties to vent, but keep the venting from becoming personal. Never allow anyone on the team to destroy anyone else.

Gather as much information as you possibly can, and get others to help you resolve the conflict. Try to do a little creative problem solving. Brainstorm ideas with the agreement that no idea is to be laughed at or trivialized. Agree on two or three ideas that seem the best to implement to solve the conflict.

It's usually good to have the conflicting parties see things from your perspective. Ask them to sit in your chair and solve the problem as if they were the leader.

Be brutally candid with yourself. Make sure you are not the problem. Make sure that you are really working at gaining mutually agreed upon solutions, and not bulldozing points, cutting off discussions, or forcing ideas. Admit it when you find yourself to be the cause of problems and conflicts. Make sure your ego isn't getting in the way.

FRAMING REALITY

Every time you introduce a new idea, you will open yourself up to criticism, second-guessing and resistance. But introducing and implementing change is a critical part of your responsibility.

Spend a lot of time framing the introduction of any change. Spend a lot of time framing the explanations of the change throughout the change process. Bring members of your team together to discuss the changes prior to announcing them to the entire group. Get others to help you frame the change in a way the team can accept it.

It's simple to frame the change in a logical, objective manner, and it is important that you do so, but it's just as important to consider the feelings of the people involved in the change. If you can't frame the change message with benefits to those involved, you've got a lousy frame. In other words statistics are fine, but emotion is critical.

Taking the time to frame issues in a positive manner, where people understand what's in it for them, will go a long way to eliminating the conflicts that come with change.

THE HARD PART

Conflict will happen. You must be aware of it and be proactive in handling it. You must be sensitive as to the consequences of your actions during and after the conflict.

In an ideal situation, you would sit down with the conflicting parties; brainstorm and problem solve, and come up with solutions that are a win for both parties. But it's rarely that easy.

Since most conflicts are less than ideal, a common solution would be for you to sit and be the judge and final solution maker. While this may seem fair, one of the parties will feel that they got the short end of the stick, and feel it was because of you.

And so we come to the hard part. The most effective, difficult and time-consuming way to handle conflict is to be a facilitator. Listen, call a time out when emotions get too high, bring in a third party when nothing else is working, look for the pluses and minuses in both parties' points of view, to record ideas on a piece of paper, to problem solve, and then be willing to scrap it all and start facilitating all over again.

When you take the time to facilitate instead of judge the conflict, you are on your way to effectively managing the conflict.

A FEW HINTS

Conflicts are rarely easy to resolve, but here are eight ideas that may make it easier.

1.   Always be aware of how your own behavior is contributing to the conflict. We are often quick to point to the other side as the instigator of the conflict, but if you're fair, your own behavior is often a major contributor. What about you? How does your behavior help or hinder in conflict situations?

2.   Be willing to work in gray areas. Conflict is rarely about right or wrong, it's usually about judgment, feelings, emotions and interpretations. What you say and do makes sense to you, and what the other side says and does makes just as much sense to them. Both sides believe they are right and tend to dig in. So if you want to resolve conflict, spend most of your time understanding and questioning, and not as much time talking and persuading.

3.   Stay calm. Never escalate a conflict because you are losing control. If you find yourself losing it, apologize and ask for a break.

4.   Watch your words. Expect that you will be misinterpreted; it will happen often in a conflict. Work to keep a positive frame. Avoid the words "always" and "never." They ignite defensiveness. Work to keep the word "but" to a minimum, it negates any positives you may bring up. Substitute the word "and" whenever possible. Watching your words is never easy. Bad habits are tough to break.

5.   Watch the blame game. People hate to be blamed for things. If you start placing fault on the other side, you will escalate the conflict. Denial and defensiveness will become the norm. The other side will rationalize or try

to place the blame back on you. Looking to blame the other will just deepen the conflict. Avoid blaming anyone for what is going wrong. Just look for solutions.

6. Look for hidden messages. What the other side is thinking and feeling is usually more important than what they are saying. Try to step back, observe and question, and figure out what the real intentions of the other person are. Your powers of observation are strong, but most people rarely put that too effective use. Be aware.

7. Spend a lot of time defining what the problem really is. We tend to jump to solutions too quickly. Instead, spend time defining what is probably a messy and complicated situation. Focus on the realities. Focusing on the problem first, really dissecting it, will help you gain great insights into a workable solution.

8. Think through the situation as if you were going to be a third party mediator. How would you mediate this situation?

The cornerstone of emotional intelligence is self-awareness. Rarely is this truer than in resolving conflicts.

BE CONSTRUCTIVE

Many conflicts become destructive and this does no one any good. Here are a couple of ideas on how to keep the conflict constructive.

*   Don't let conflicts fester; address them.
*   Ask the other person to give you some ideas on how to handle the conflict.
*   Don't use inflammatory remarks. You will just escalate the conflict.
*   Stay away from sarcasm. Be real and be honest.
*   When things get out of control, take a time out.
*   Watch exaggerating your position. A smart person will jump all over you when you do this.
*   Keep as calm as possible.

- Be aware of a suitable solution, and allow it to take the place of a perfect solution.

- Keep your ego in control.

- Watch your language. It's your responsibility to make sure that the communication is clear and accurately received.

- Don't ever use personal attacks.

- Prepare whenever you can before going into a conflicting situation,

These are a few things to be aware of, and some should help. Even when you are at your best the conflicting situation will be one of your greatest challenges. And you may not believe it at the time, but it will also be one of your greatest learning opportunities.

12

NEGOTIATION

NEEDS

It's really interesting to watch people in a seminar participate in a simple negotiation role-play. Each "negotiator" is given a scenario where if they can acquire some rare apples, they can produce a serum that can prevent a major epidemic. They have the same resources, and both need all the apples they can get.

As the negotiation goes on, the participants get very involved in their own position. They want and need all the apples to solve their problem. However, they miss an important point. One group needs the juice of the apple; the other needs the skin. If the participants would just focus on what they need rather than on their positions, they would have a pretty easy negotiation. But they don't, and the sorry truth is that most negotiators miss this point, and thus miss a most important negotiation fundamental: focus on needs, not positions.

Start a negotiation by taking the time to separate your needs from your positions. You will find that there are a number of positions available that will allow you to meet your particular needs.

You will also benefit by taking time to identify the other persons needs and interests. Do your homework carefully and calmly. Try to put yourself in the other persons' shoes and think the negotiation through.

Remember, **put your needs ahead of your position.**

POWER

Having more power than the other person does not mean you will be successful in a negotiating situation, but it helps. Here are some examples of power that a negotiator may have:

- Authority: Do you have the authority to close the deal? Do you have more authority than the other person does?

- Money: Is money the issue? Who has it? Who is trying to get it?

- Right: Who has "right" on their side? Do you have the law on your side?

- Deadlines: Who has time on their side? Do you know your opponent's time frame? Will you be able to remain calm as your deadline approaches?

- Knowledge: What do you know? How much information do you have on the other party? Where can you get more information if you need it?

- Proficiency: Are you an expert in this area? Is your opponent? Can you get expertise on your side?

- Walk-away: Are you willing to walk away with no solution? Is the other party willing to walk?

Having power does not mean you will be successful in your negotiations. Just think about how many car salespeople win when the buyer really has all the power in his or her favor. Know your power base, and be willing to use it.

FEAR

If you go into a negotiation with a lot of fear, you're likely to fail. You need to have the courage to be rejected, have the courage to be vulnerable, have the courage to walk away from a deal. It is the people who have the courage to face their apprehensions with courage and confidence that make the best negotiators.

SUCCESS GUIDELINES

You can never be sure that you will be successful in a negotiation, but here are a few ideas that will help.

- Be patient, listen, take your time.
- Be candid without giving up too much information.
- Keep your emotions in check.
- Stay positive and professional.
- Get the other person saying "yes" often.
- Keep notes.
- Get the other person to state his or her demands first.
- Test your opponent. You never know what he or she will concede.
- Don't act too smart or too sophisticated.
- Ask a lot of questions.
- Check all information.
- Don't ignore the other's position, but work hard to identify their real needs.
- Watch the words "but" and "however." Effective negotiators use these words to their advantage.
- Trust your instincts when things don't smell right.
- Ask for help when you need it.
- Keep your time frame to yourself.
- Don't get stuck on one approach. Be flexible.

PREPARE WELL

As a negotiation comes near, you need to do some preparation. Take some time to fully prepare, and you won't regret it. These questions should help.

- What are your objectives?
- What are you trying to accomplish?

- What are your needs?

- What do you know about the situation?

- How can you get more information?

- What do you know about the other party?

- Who has power?

- Who has right on their side?

- What are the deadlines?

- Who are the decision-makers?

- Are there legal matters involved?

- Do you know the other side's needs, interests, hot buttons?

- How will you present your case?

- How will you encourage the other to engage in a real two-way discussion?

- Are you focused and ready?

- Do you have any necessary material or documents?

- Are you focused on winning or are you focused on both sides coming out ahead?

You can never prepare enough for an important negotiation.

GETTING TO YES

One of the best books ever written on Negotiation has to be *Getting to Yes*. In it Roger Fisher, Bruce Patton and William Ury have taken their research from the Harvard Negotiation Project and developed a principled way to approach leadership. One of the most powerful concepts is BATNA. [9]

BATNA stands for your Best Alternative To a Negotiated Agreement. Taking the time during your preparation time to identify your BATNA is crucial to your success as a negotiator. Good negotiators know what will happen if no negotiation is reached. Great negotiators know the best alternative they have in their pocket before the negotiation begins.

Ask yourself: What will happen if no agreement is reached during the negotiation? Is this my best alternative, or is there a better one? What is the other side's best alternative?

Having a strong BATNA will help you make a good decision. Not having one might leave you worse off than you should be.

COLLABORATE

After you prepare, you know a lot about your negotiation stance, but not nearly enough about the other side's real needs. It's important to share information that can identify things that can benefit the negotiation, but are not real obvious. Negotiations are rarely as successful as they can be when it is a "me against you" scenario.

Collaborate and you will identify real value that isn't readily apparent. For example, if you go to buy a house you like, and just focus on haggling over a price; you may miss some additional points. You may not recognize that the person moving out is moving to the city and has no need for her car, and you need a car. You might not recognize that she will need to store some furniture, and you have a place to store it. You may not realize a lot of things because you didn't ask. You were not collaborative.

To set up a collaborative negotiation, you may say:

> "I think it would be good if we took a little time early on making sure that we both know where we are coming from. Why don't we both give our perception of the negotiation? You could start by giving your view. I will ask some questions to make sure I understand your view. Then I could give my view, and you could ask me some questions to make sure you understand where I am coming from. Is that O.K. with you?"

The more collaborative you can become, the more you can focus on the real needs. You will identify new areas of value to each party, and the negotiation will be less likely to become hostile.

TACTICS

Experienced negotiators may use different tactics, gambits, or ploys against you during a negotiation. Being aware of these tactics will help you minimize the effectiveness they may have. Here are some of the most common tactics.

- Good guy/bad guy: One of the most famous of tactics. It is effective even when you know it is being used. When one person is very aggressive while the other nice and reasonable be on the defensive. Don't be seduced by the good guy.

- Higher authority: This is a most effective tactic. The other party agrees to a solution, but says that he or she must take it to a boss or committee for approval. Don't be surprised when the other party comes back and tells you that the committee won't approve the offer and you have to do better.

  Always play to the other person's ego if they pull the "higher authority" gambit. Ask them if they are going to personally recommend the offer to the committee by saying; "You will recommend this to the committee, won't you?"

- First offer: Jump at the first offer only when it is too good to pass up. Always try to get the other party to make the first offer.

- The written proposal: Negotiators like to submit a written proposal, and ask you to sign it and get it back to them by a certain date. If you don't like the proposal, send them a counterproposal in writing, and ask them to sign it and send it back to you.

- Take it or leave it: This is usually just a threat, so don't stand for it. Ask the other why they are using this tactic. Be prepared to "leave" it.

- You will have to do better: Ask "why or exactly how do we have to do better?" Focus on why your proposal is fair. Look for small concessions you can make, while at the same time look for some reciprocal trade-offs.

- Non-verbals: Negotiators plan a "flinch" every now and then to put you on the defensive about your offer. Watch your own non-verbals, or you will give a lot of information away.

- Feel/felt/found: This is a good technique for handling objections. It goes like this: "I understand how you <u>feel</u>, many people have <u>felt</u> the same way, but our new research <u>found</u> that...."

- Split the difference: Only do this when both parties will benefit.

- Personal attack: Keep your cool, and let the other person vent. But there is no reason why you have to accept the attack. If there is a real personality clash, you may want to bring in someone else to conclude the negotiation.

BE YOURSELF

There are few rules to effective negotiation. Your style is probably as effective as anyone else's. Negotiation is not about how smart you are. It is about gathering information, communicating, listening, keeping your cool, and making a smart deal.

Know yourself and be yourself. Know how you feel about the negotiation, because both your positive and negative feelings will come through. Negotiation is a sophisticated form of communication, and when you are thinking and acting with a positive attitude, you will have a better chance of succeeding.

13

DELEGATION

EMPOWERMENT

The idea of "empowering" employees is one of the more popular subjects in management today. It is being talked about as some new idea whose time has come.

But great managers have been empowering employees for years through excellent delegation. They have always appreciated the value of their team, and had the courage to trust them with responsibility, authority and accountability. In other words, they empowered them.

You will always be faced with reconciling the fine line between your responsibility and letting go. You will always be concerned with the paradox of the more you give up, the more you accomplish. You will probably never be comfortable when you give up some control, but you must do it if you want to lead.

Most managers say they delegate a lot already, but most employees would disagree. When tasks are handed out, a lot of emphasis is placed on how the task should be accomplished, little on why the task is important. Over control is not delegation, and it is not empowerment, but it is a common management technique.

Evaluate what and how you delegate. Great leaders have great followers who accomplish extraordinary results. Delegate effectively and your followers will have a chance to flourish.

BENEFITS

Delegation is good management and it benefits you and your team in many ways, including:

- Better results: Given your time and pressure constraints, you certainly can't do it all and expect to get extraordinary results. But your followers can, so delegate real work to them.

- Better productivity: Delegation leverages your time, but it also raises the morale and self esteem of your team. Give them important, challenging work and watch them flourish.

- Better development: Delegation helps develop a skilled working team. It also helps you to identify future superstars and management talent.

Delegation and leadership are similar in many ways. In both cases many of the skills are instinctive, while others are rarely natural. You need to make a conscious effort to be a good delegator, because it is one of the less natural of the leadership skills.

RATIONALIZATION

"Now wait a minute, I don't have time; I'll do it myself."

"My team just doesn't have the skill; I'll have to do it myself."

"Senior management told me to do it."

"I can do it better."

"I am the expert."

Do any of these statements sound like you? If they do, watch out, because you are rationalizing why things cannot be delegated.

Team leaders and managers need to delegate. It takes courage and trust to delegate important tasks to someone else, but you must. When you delegate properly, you will not lose total control, and you will gain the respect of those you work with.

When you give your team important responsibilities, you are saying loud and clear that you trust them and expect them to do great things. When you fail to give them challenges, you are telling them just the opposite.

Role clarity is critical to team success, and some tasks will flow naturally to certain people on the team, but be careful. It's easy to fall into a rut, and continually delegate the same things to the same people over and over again.

Evaluate your team. Know their strengths and weaknesses. Make sure you are not falling into the rut of giving the same type of tasks to the same people all the time. Not only will these people start getting a little bored with tasks that start to become a little routine, you will miss the opportunity to give someone else a valuable learning experience.

DUMPING

Many managers and team leaders think they are great at delegating, while what they are really good at is dumping. They take tasks they hate doing and dump them on their team.

There is a big difference between delegating and dumping. When you surround yourself with great people, you need to challenge them with meaningful and important work. Delegation happens when you determine the important tasks that need to be done, identify the proper people to carry out the assignment, tell them what needs to be accomplished, and why it needs to be accomplished, and then let them go do the job.

Delegation includes giving responsibility, proper authority, and strong accountability. In other words, delegation is trust.

COMMUNICATE

There is no one best way to delegate, but here are a few good thoughts to get you started.

- After choosing the right people to delegate to, meet with them to discuss the assignment. Give a clear overview of what it is you want accomplished, and have high expectations for the results. Tell the team why you want the assignment accomplished, and give them as much information on the task as possible. Ask them what their thoughts are, and make sure they clarify any concerns they may have. Let them know that you will be available if they need your help, but encourage them to make their own decisions.

- Find ways to customize each delegation. Consider the abilities, needs, and readiness of the person you are delegating to. Make sure you get the delegatee to summarize the assignment to you to make sure there is agreement as to the task goals and deadlines.

- Establish a follow-up procedure and stick to it. Set up a tickler file to remind you of important deadlines. But be careful, don't jump in and assume control unless absolutely necessary.

- Don't forget to recognize the hard work and accomplishments. Thank the people and make sure they get credit for the results of the job.

PERFECT FLOW

Wouldn't it be great if all the tasks you delegate get accomplished without a hitch? But like all human endeavors, it's usually a little messy. Expect the best, but be ready for the mess. Be ready to intervene, but also be careful not to take over unless it is absolutely necessary. When in doubt, take a chance and let the delegatee continue with the task. The chances you take with your best people will pay huge dividends in the future. The trust and learning experience will be invaluable.

14

MEETINGS

TRADITION

It must be tradition that keeps us going to meeting after meaningless meeting. One of the great mysteries of life is why can't there be fewer and more productive meetings. I'm sure you all resent the amount of time you waste at meetings. If you ever keep a log of how you spend your time, don't be surprised if you find the greatest portion of your unproductive time is spent in meetings.

Don't be the person who continues this tradition of endless and pointless meetings. You should be the exception, and run meetings that are beneficial and productive.

The key questions to ask, and ask often are:

- Do we need this meeting?
- Is a meeting the best method to meet our need or accomplish our goal?
- What are the alternatives to a meeting?
- Is there a better way to handle this situation than to have a meeting?

Hold meetings only when the participants will learn something or be moved to action. The exception to this rule is to hold a meeting for recognition purposes. Go into every meeting with a philosophy that the attendees will leave better off than when they came in.

Always think about who should attend. Invite only those who are critical to the meeting's outcome, or those who will really benefit from attending. Think about those you may offend by leaving them out.

Avoid the regular meeting habit. Tradition says there are legitimate reasons to hold regular meetings, but challenge tradition. Don't hold a meeting on Tuesday morning just because you always have in the past.

Get your team leaders to help you make your meetings better. Ask them how they feel about the meetings. Ask them to run the next few meetings, to set the agenda, be presenters and bring in outsiders. Ask them how you could add value to your meetings. If your team recommends you not hold a meeting, don't hold it.

Keep your meetings short. People rarely complain about meetings that end early. They do complain about meetings that go too long.

PREPARATION

Your chances of running a successful meeting always increase when you spend time preparing for it. Write down your objectives and the outcomes that you expect from the meeting. Prepare an agenda and distribute it. Include the time and place, and any special preparation that will be needed by the participants.

Find adequate meeting space. Make sure everyone will be comfortable, and make sure the space has the equipment you need.

Practice any formal presentations you intend to make. Don't wing it. And anticipate objections.

Prepare visual aids before time. Make sure all the equipment is tested before you start.

Prepare handouts for the meeting, and have enough for everyone.

Build in time for recognition whenever you can. Give credit to others, recognize achievements. Keep the meeting as positive as possible.

Keep administrative details that can be covered in a memo or e-mail out of your meetings whenever possible.

Limit interruptions, especially when you are holding the meeting in your office. If you expect to be interrupted, let the participants know about it before the meeting starts.

Be prepared to summarize the meeting, and to distribute the summary to others who attended the meeting.

BE A FACILITATOR

The best meetings happen when real ideas are exchanged and action agreed upon. This only happens when the leader is a facilitator. Learn to facilitate, not dominate your meetings. Facilitation encourages others to fully participate without feeling threatened or intimidated. Domination encourages others to be reluctant, resistant, detached and patronizing.

To be an effective facilitator, you need to be able to get a discussion going, keep it going and keep the meeting focused on the main points.

To get the discussion going, position the meeting so that the participants are clear as to the topic, objectives and benefits to them. When you invite them to the meeting, make sure that they know that you expect them to be active and open participants. Over time you won't have to ask people to be active participants, but early on you should.

To keep the discussion going in a meeting, use a lot of open probes to see what ideas the group has. Support the answers unless they are way off track. Ask for opinions, clarifications, summaries and examples. Keep your own ideas short and supportive. There will always be a time for your final thoughts and opinions.

The group will try to find out where you stand on issues, and you will want to tell them. If you do, they will pick up on your ideas and either patronize you or resist your ideas. Try not to give your view early. Re-direct any questions and comments addressed to you back to the participants. It's amazing how many times they will come up with a better answer than you would have. While you shouldn't evade any direct questions, try not to be the first to answer.

Be ready to stop the discussion from going off track. Summarizing ideas from time to time is a good way to re-focus the group. Summarizing also allows you to put emphasis on key areas, and it is a terrific way to end a meeting.

To keep the main points alive, capture ideas on a flip chart or some other visible note-taking vehicle. Support relevant remarks, and tactfully bring digressions back to the main topic. Ask for clarification when there is some confusion as to where the participant is taking the discussion.

Listen carefully and always keep your emotions in check. Be positive, and work to keep your energy level up. Being a good facilitator will take a lot out of you.

DISCORD

Not all meetings go without a hitch. Conflicts do come up, and how you handle them will go a long way in determining whether or not the meeting will be a success.

When dealing with conflict, keep your emotions in check. Work hard at getting the entire group involved. When a strong difference is voiced that seem to be leading toward conflict, ask the entire group how they feel about the idea.

There are times when you need to directly confront a difficult difference of opinion. Be up front about your feelings, and work to resolve the issue by logical data and common sense. And always realize that common sense will not overcome strong emotions. Be ready to reframe ideas in a more positive manner when emotions overcome rationality.

When things get out of hand, it is often best to table a difficult issue. The conflict still remains and must be dealt with, but by tabling the issues you give yourself and others time to calm down and rethink positions and ideas.

You can always use your power and crush any conflict, but this will probably turn off the entire group, and will hurt you in the long run. Being viewed as someone who will use power when necessary can intimidate others. You don't want to be viewed as the intimidator. Use your power wisely.

Try to get the entire group to address conflict by generating alternatives. Ask a lot of questions and record the answers on a flip chart. Brainstorm and pick out the best ideas. Try to bring the emotion level down when things get intense. Allow for the expression of strong statements, but try to keep the over-emotional expressions to a minimum. Most importantly, keep your emotions in check.

If the meeting gets out of hand, take a break. Take the person responsible for the conflict aside and explain what is happening, and what it means to the overall success or failure of the meeting. Ask some questions on how to resolve the conflict. Listen carefully and try to recognize any underlying problems that led to the conflict, problems that you will need to address at another time. Keep this discussion private.

Finally, if you are comfortable using humor, use it. Humor is often a release, and can give you some needed time to get the meeting back on track.

A CHECKLIST

Think through your next meeting. Here is a checklist to help:

- Define the goals and objective
- Prepare an agenda
- Identify participants/confirm attendance
- Arrange for meeting space
- Order materials
- Check audio-visual requirements
- Identify who is going to control the meeting
- Order refreshments, if appropriate
- Start and end on time
- Encourage participation

- Be candid, but sensitive
- Listen more than talk
- Summarize ideas/Stay on track
- Insist on closure
- Follow-up on action items
- Brief others on the meeting's outcome

15

TERMINATION

SOME THOUGHTS

No matter how good a leader you are, you will have people that are just not making it in the job they have. You work with them, coach them, counsel them, and when all else fails, you have the responsibility to fire them.

Termination is one of the most difficult responsibilities of a manager. It's not the fun part of the job, but it's often a necessary part of the job. It's something that you will probably have to do at some point in your managerial career.

Always terminate people for the right reasons. Firing people for the wrong reason, such as you simply don't like them, will get you in a lot of trouble. Lawyers love wrongful termination suits.

It's interesting how things improve when you fire someone who deserved to be terminated. You send a clear message that certain behaviors will not be tolerated. You send a clear message that your area is dedicated to only the highest standards. Morale gets better, because people feel a sense of pride when they work in a high achieving, ethical workplace.

Many managers fear that if they terminate someone, they will face a lawsuit. Never fear a lawsuit if you terminated someone the correct way for the correct reasons.

PROBATION

Probation is a funny thing. Most people on probation improve enough to just get off it. If you are putting someone on probation, have him or her write their own improvement plan, and you approve it. If they continue to fail, they are failing to meet their own promises, and it is easier to terminate them.

WHY TERMINATE

There are many valid reasons to terminate; let's look at a few:

- Consistently poor performance
- Gross misconduct
- Lying
- Negligence
- Insubordination
- Poor attitude that brings others down
- Sexual harassment
- Stealing
- Physical violence
- Illegal activities

PREPARATION

When you make the final decision to terminate a member of your team, it's best to act quickly. At the same time you must be thoroughly prepared. Think about the following:

- Ask yourself: Have I done everything possible to solve this problem?
- Assemble all the facts you can (written notices, performance appraisals, complaint letters, coaching notes, etc.)
- Prepare information regarding pay, benefits, unpaid vacation or severance.
- Organize the reasons for the termination in your mind.
- Decide on when and where the meeting will take place.

- Check to make sure the termination date is not a special occasion (birthday, anniversary, etc.)

- Rehearse what you are going to say.

- Determine if someone else should accompany you for legal or possibly safety reasons.

THE TERMINATION MEETING

Try to keep the termination meeting short. As you open the meeting get right to the point. Terminate the person within the first few minutes. Avoid small talk. Do not become apologetic, and don't lay the blame on someone else. In a straightforward way tell the person he or she has been terminated.

Listen and respond factually. Don't get defensive, and stay away from arguments. Avoid personal attacks by focusing on the behavior and performance reasons for the termination. Keep on track; avoid issues that are irrelevant to the termination.

Try not to get emotional. Avoid saying things such as, "This isn't the worst thing that can happen to you."

Don't let the employee get you to change your mind. Resolve any final matters such as compensation or vacation time earned. Try to get the employee focused on the future. Stay in control and make no promises you can't keep. End the meeting in a business like manner.

When you have done a good job of managing, the termination will not come as much of a surprise. Some people will be hurt and angry, others may be relieved. Most people will focus on what you are prepared to do for them. Always be ready to discuss the next step.

WHAT TO EXPECT

Never guess how someone will react to the news they have been terminated. Never be surprised. Here are a few common reactions:

KNEW IT WAS COMING: This is a common reaction. If you have done your job well, you have given sufficient notice that the termination was coming. Most people have been expecting it and are actually relieved the process is over.

SHOCK: Here the person fired just sits and stares at you. The person is not facing up to reality, and is not O.K.

You have to make sure this person understands what just happened. Ask them some questions. Get them to focus on the next steps. Be patient with this person during the termination because the person terminated is going through a traumatic experience.

HOSTILITY: Some people overreact by yelling, screaming and even threatening bodily harm. The person may lash out at you and the company, and may threaten to sue. They will challenge your right to fire them, and make allegations of unfairness.

Don't get into an argument with the hostile person. Let the person vent, and don't get intimidated. When challenged, calmly go back to the factual reasons for the termination. Don't get defensive, most people will eventually calm down.

DEPRESSION: You might get a reaction like: "How can this be happening to me?" or, "It's just not fair; what will I ever do now?" These are reactions of hurt pride and depression. The person being terminated is embarrassed and doesn't want to face his or her peers.

Try to get this person focused on the future, and on the next steps. Also find a way to get this person out of the office in a way they won't be embarrassed.

RETREAT: This person wants to get out of the office as fast as possible. They will internalize their feelings, and once they leave they will be very vocal about you and the dismissal.

There is not much you can do about this person except to try to get him or her to vent their feelings before they leave.

CAUTION

Lawyers feast on managers who terminate employees for the wrong reasons. Managers who fire employees because of age, religion or sex are particularly vulnerable. The wearisome and expensive lawsuit that follows takes an enormous amount of emotional energy, and could lead to a long-term reputation problem.

The possibility of a lawsuit should not stop you from terminating an employee for the right reasons. As long as you practice good management, you will have a strong case against any lawsuit brought against you.

Whenever you observe a behavior that could lead to eventual termination, immediately sit down with the employee and discuss the problem. Mutually agree upon a solution. When problems continue, sit down with the employee and put the corrective action down in writing. Follow this with a formal written warning, letting the employee know that the next step will be dismissal.

Good practices may not prevent a lawsuit, but they will put you on solid ground during any proceedings. Treating people fairly will always keep you a step ahead.

16

MANAGING FOR PROFITABILITY

BUSINESS PHILOSOPHY

The profit chain is made up of many small and some not so small links. You and your team make up one of those links, and it is important for you to focus on how to make your team one of the strong links in the chain.

Managing for profitability is not necessarily the fun part of the business, and usually is not the typical manager's strong point. But it should be. For organizations to flourish, managers, team leaders and even team members should think like business people. The mindset you should have is:

"If this were my business, would I run it this way?"

Managing for profitability is part awareness and part common sense. It all starts with having a strong philosophy that you can impart to others.

To develop a business philosophy, look around and observe what is happening in the workplace. Reflect on what is changing, because things change at a rapid pace. Reflect on how you and your team are functioning. Reflect on how you might want to improve the way you do things. Taking the time to sit back and reflect is very important, and it is a common practice among leaders at all levels. It will be time well spent.

Become an expert in your business by being curious. Understand your industry, your competition, and how things are changing around you. Focus on your clients, and how your team can play a role in better client satisfaction. Constantly challenge the status quo, never get complacent.

Building a solid business philosophy is a key step in managing for profitability. Living the philosophy is the critical step.

LONG TERM

The principal reason any company stays in business is that it meets the needs of its customers with products and services that make sense. Clients reward these efforts by giving us enough revenue to exceed our costs. Maximizing ethical profits is the job of every team member, but few view their job in that manner. You must.

Customers are smart, and they are getting more and more alternatives to choose from every day. Customization to meet client needs, the way they want them met, is the future for all businesses. The only problem is that the future is today, and clients will leave you if you can't continually customize your products and services to meet their needs.

If you are solely focused on making a short-term profit, you will find it very difficult to change to the customized approach that clients are demanding today. The paradox that most managers face today is that they have to get profits today while still building for the long term, but if you do things right, you will likely be successful in getting both. And as a leader, you will be expected to do both.

The key questions you need to ask are:

- Are we meeting our clients' needs?
- Are we exceeding their needs?
- What will it take to exceed their needs?
- What do we need to do to retain our clients?
- What will it cost us to retain our clients?
- What does it cost us to get a new client?

- What does a profitable client look like?
- What are we doing to retain key employees?
- How can we keep our cash flow positive?

You should think about the ramifications your cost saving decisions have on the customer, key employees, and the bottom line. You should also be aware that costs could get out of whack. It's a good practice to regularly review your expenses to insure that no fat is settling in.

Always question decisions you make for the short term. Short-term decisions that hinder long term growth are rarely the decisions a real leader would make.

THE BUDGET

Budgeting will rarely make the list of your favorite things to do. It takes time, and is often a painstaking exercise, but it is a critical step in the planning cycle. It is the step that helps you focus on the resources you will have available to accomplish your goals.

Think of your team or group as your own business. As the business owner, what do you want to accomplish, how and with whom? What activities are you planning? What are your resources? What do your revenues look like? What are your fixed costs? What do you anticipate your variable costs to be? Are there creative alternatives available for you to achieve the results you envision? Question everything during the budget process.

All planning tools should be flexible, and the budget should be no different. It should be updated on a regular basis to reflect what is really happening in the workplace. It will also serve as a wonderful barometer, giving you encouragement when the news is good, and serving as a warning when things are bad.

If you have forms to fill out, they are usually accompanied by some instructions for what should be included in each category. Read these and put the proper numbers on the proper line. The instructions will normally answer a lot of your budget questions and even give you some ideas that you haven't considered. Instructions can often be your friend.

Get copies of previous budgets. Look at last year's budget and tie it into how you actually did. Look for trends that may continue into this year.

Empower someone to be responsible for monitoring the budget throughout the year. Stay involved with this person; you never want to become blindsided by some unusual occurrence.

YOUR P & L

If you get a monthly Profit and Loss (P & L) Statement, you should become proficient in reading it. It will be a relatively simple statement because it basically reports back only two things: your revenues and your expenses. It may look complicated because it will include things like depreciation, occupancy costs, allocated charges and miscellaneous expense, but if you sit down with a financial person, you can be educated in reading it in no time.

Take a few hours with the financial person to go over your P & L one line at a time. Ask a lot of questions, and stay with it until you understand the entire report. Ask about typical problem areas, and how to get errors corrected.

Spend some time with a manager you respect and compare P & L's. Compare notes on how each of you handles different expenses.

The statement itself is simple. It is based on the following equation:

REVENUES minus EXPENSES = PROFIT or (LOSS)

Not every group or team is a profit area, but everyone has expenses. So they must be watched. Review your P & L monthly. Get errors corrected quickly.

WATCHING COSTS

Your P & L will usually be backed up with details on what was expensed to your area. Have someone review this detail regularly. Mistakes often appear on these reports, and they must be corrected quickly.

Share your P & L with your team. Ask them their opinion on how critical costs that affect your area are being handled, and ask them to suggest ideas on how these costs might be handled better.

Look at each expense and question how it benefits your team, the client, and the organization. Eliminate expenses that cannot be justified.

Audit your communications and technology costs. Little costs such as extra phone lines, or unneeded computer charges sneak in, and never seem to get removed.

If you have a lease, review it. Know what you are entitled to and make sure you get it. Look at the market and if your lease is at the high end, there is no harm in reviewing it and trying to renegotiate it to get better terms.

Watch the mail, fax and travel charges. These add up fast. Watch for the "nice to have" versus the "need to have." Be disciplined. Don't let the niceties add up to a big expense.

Figure out what it costs to open your door each day. Simply take the average of your last two years' expenses and divide it by 252 (working days). This number is especially valuable if you are a revenue producing area, because it will give you a revenue goal for each day.

Being aware is the key. Be aware of costs and expenses—some are justifiable and some are wasteful. Be on the look out for ways to maximize the bottom line. Be proactive in your management of the P & L.

17

PRESENTATION SKILLS

FEAR

It sure sounded like a great opportunity when your boss asked you to speak at the National Managers Meeting. You were honored, and flattered, but now as the presentation approaches, you start to get concerned. The speech is all you think about, you're losing sleep, your staff thinks you are going crazy and "the day" keeps getting closer.

You have prepared and practiced like no other time in your life. You are as ready as you have ever been. But now, as you are about to go on, you start to panic. Your hands are sweaty, your mouth is dry, and you have a queasy feeling in your stomach. Your heart is racing, and you wish you were anywhere but where you are. You just know that the audience is going to hate what you have to say. As you are being introduced, your fear of failure is at its peak.

The fear of public speaking is very common. According to research, more than twice as many people fear speaking before a group, than fear death. But even if you are one of the many who fear public speaking, there are really very few reasons why you can't be good at it.

The skills needed to be an effective speaker are not fancy. With practice, they can be learned.

EYE CONTACT

The one skill you need to master is eye contact. It's been said that the eyes are the gateway to the mind, and when it comes to presentations nothing could be truer. Whatever the eyes take in, the mind will focus on. Whatever the mind focuses on will be reflected in the quality of the presentation. The key to any good presentation is how it comes across to your audience, and it is through the eyes that you will start to build credibility with your audience. Audiences liked to be looked at.

When your eyes focus on things other than your audience, excess information enters your brain. This will effect your concentration, and distract you. The extra stimulus entering your thought process will have a negative effect on your overall presentation. So, not only is eye contact the most powerful means you have to establish rapport and credibility with your audience, it is the main reason why you will be able to stay focused on what you have to say.

Your eyes are your most important feature. Your smile, gestures and physical movements all start with the eyes. Eye contact is the most important of the skills to master if you are to become a great presenter.

FOCUSING

When making your presentation, looking directly at one person at a time is critical.

Make your presentation a series of one-on one conversations.

Pick out a person and look right into their eyes for an entire thought (3-6 seconds). Talk directly to that person, and then move on to another pair of eyes for your next thought.

Make sure you focus on people in different areas of the audience. Watch for a bias to one side of the room. If you have the tendency to focus on one side over the other, try angling your body to the side you tend to ignore. This should help you get to the area you usually miss, while still allowing you to get to the side you prefer.

When speaking to a large group, break the group into quadrants. Pick out a few friendly faces in each quadrant and make eye contact with them. The rest of the quadrant will feel that you have also made contact with them. Be careful not to spend too much time in one area; the entire audience is important.

Your eyes will always give you away. By increasing the quality of your eye contact, you will increase the quality of your presentations. Practice it often.

TOTAL IMPACT

The seminal research of Dr. Albert Mehrabian is probably the most quoted work when it comes to communication. Professor Mehrabian found that the total impact of your message is only 7% words, 38% tone and 55% non-verbal. 93% comes from your eye contact, body language and tone of your voice—93%! Most of you probably spend hours writing the words and only minutes practicing the delivery. [10]

Stop spending all your time perfecting your words. Spend it perfecting your delivery.

TENSION

Every time you make a speech your adrenaline will start to increase, and you will have a lot of energy to expend. You will be a little anxious, a little nervous, and believe it or not this is exactly the way you need to feel. Your nervous energy is not only normal, it can be helpful.

Great speakers often talk about getting nervous before a presentation. Just like you, they get the dry throat and sweaty palms. And they know from experience that as long as they prepare well, their nervousness will start to give way to positive energy soon after the presentation begins.

Take a few minutes before you speak and visualize an audience that is looking forward to hearing your message. Visualize yourself as a confident speaker, one who has something valuable to impart. Take a number of real deep breaths, deep from your stomach not your chest. Let the air out slowly and repeat the breathing as you visualize yourself making a great presentation.

Learning the proper way to move and gesture will also reduce your nervousness because it is often the physical skills that make us the most self-conscious.

MOVEMENT

Are you concerned about the following as you make your presentations:

- What should I do with my hands?

- Why do I look so awkward?

- Is my voice O.K.?

- Are my movements appropriate?

Physical skills are totally individual. Some of you love to move around, and some of you would prefer to stay in one place. Some will gesture a lot, some very little. The main rule of movement is "everything in moderation."

If you find that you move around too much or that you move too quickly, your audience may find you to be distracting. If you sway from one foot to the other, your audience may get a little queasy.

To eliminate movement, plant your feet about shoulder width apart and try to limit your movement to the upper part of your body. You won't totally eliminate your movement with this stance, but you will moderate it, and this is your real goal.

Too little movement can also be a distraction. You don't want to be a talking statue. You need to have a little movement. Become aware of how you move during your presentations

Often a podium or some similar device is a crutch to the non-mover. Be aware that clutching a podium will not eliminate your nervousness or help the audience understand your points. It's not wrong to use a podium, but don't hold on to it. Step back a little from the podium and try to gesture naturally. This little hint is critical, especially if you are afraid to move around.

Moving in and out of your audience is a personal preference. If you are comfortable with this, and if the setting is right, then move into the audience. If you are not comfortable with it, don't do it. One thing to remember is that when you move into the audience, your back is what part of the audience is seeing, not your eyes. So make sure you move back to the front regularly so the whole audience can see that you are paying attention to them.

VOICE

Have you ever tape recorded yourself and heard your voice for the first time? What a shock it is. You would never believe that your voice sounds like it does.

Most of us are shocked when we hear our voice, and most of us are not pleased with its sound. However, most vocal tone will be at a level that neither thrills, nor offends your audience. What does excite an audience is a voice that can be clearly heard and one that varies in pitch and speed. What turns them off is the low energy monotone speaker.

Tape-record some of your presentations and focus on how you are modulating your voice. Work to insure that you are not a monotone speaker. Practicing with a tape recorder will give you instant feedback. Practice projecting. Practice adding to your pitch and pace.

GESTURES

Many presenters have a problem with their hands. When you put your hands in your pockets, or behind your back, or locked at your side, you will usually appear robot like and nervous. When you loosen up and trust your instincts, your gestures will come more naturally.

If you are having trouble with your gestures, try bending your arms at the elbow and keeping them out in front of you. When you combine this posture with solid eye contact, your gestures will come more naturally.

Some common mistakes you want to avoid include:

- The fig leaf position—hand clasped in front of you.
- Finger pointing.
- Coin jingling—take all coins and keys out of your pockets before the presentation.

- Grasping a lectern or the back of a chair.
- Conflicting gestures—putting two fingers up when you are making four points.
- Parade rest position—hands clasped behind you.
- Arms folded in front of you

VIDEOTAPE YOURSELF

If you have the opportunity to video your practice and/or your live presentation, do it. The feedback you get from seeing yourself is invaluable.

When reviewing the video, look for the positives first. The tendency will be to be very critical of yourself, and that is not always the best approach. You will always find the negatives and you will want to eliminate anything that is ruining the presentation, but it is the positive characteristics that will make you a great presenter. Focus on what you do right first.

When reviewing the tape, look for:
- Comfort and energy
- Voice quality
- Movement—excessive/too little/swaying/shuffling/pacing
- Eye contact versus roving or darting eyes
- Posture
- Facial expression
- Gestures

Ask yourself:
- How did it go?
- Did my opener grab the audience?
- What is my strongest attribute?
- Next strongest?
- Weakest attribute?

- What can I do to improve?

- Did I make a convincing presentation?

- Was my ending strong?

Use the stop/start method of reviewing the tape. Review a few minutes of the tape and write down a few things you did well and a few things you want to work on. Play a few more minutes and do the same thing. Play a few minutes with the sound off to observe your eye contact, gestures and other non-verbals.

Reviewing tapes of yourself with a coach is even more effective, but not always practical. At the very least review the tape alone.

ORGANIZING THE PRESENTATION

Great presentations start with solid preparation. Preparation starts with knowing your subject and knowing your audience.

Start with a general idea of your subject, identify the theme of your presentation, and do your homework. Research areas that support your theme. Go to the library, search the Internet, look at in house publications, and talk to experts. No matter how much you know about a particular subject, you can learn more.

Find out about your audience. Think about their needs, values, and knowledge of the subject. When thinking about your audience, consider the following:

- Knowledgeable/little knowledge

- Age/experience

- Tough/easy

- Size of the group

- Hostile/friendly/neutral/apathetic

- Expectations—high/low/none

- Underlying feelings that could get in the way

- Know you/don't know you

- Who is on before you

- Timing of the presentation
- Receptivity to your subject matter

After starting with a theme that meets your particular audience's needs, you will want to prepare a presentation to meet those needs.

Your opening is critical. You will have about a minute to make a good impression and grab the audience's attention. Avoid the "I'm happy to be here" opening, and look for something more creative. Quotes, an appropriate joke, a clip from a famous movie are all different but effective ways to get your audience involved. Practice your opening until it is smooth and effective.

The main part of your presentation should be full of anecdotes, analogies, examples stories, statistics and personal experiences to back up your overall theme. The more you can make your presentation a conversation, the more you can make it a story—the more effective it will be.

Use humor, but only if you are good at it. Keep your information as simple and as relevant as you can.

Plan your close. Most presenters forget this important task and look foolish as they try to end the presentation. Don't let this happen to you. Prepare a strong close, thank the audience and sit down.

VISUAL AIDS

Information is easier to remember when we use more of our senses. Research has shown that 83% of all information we receive and store come through our eyes. Visual aids can really help your presentation.

A few things to think about as you develop you visuals are:

- The size of the audience
- Your budget
- Meeting atmosphere
- What other presenters are using

- Your comfort level with slides, computer visuals, audio, video, overheads, props, flipcharts, handouts, etc.

- The room set up—including the proper set up for PowerPoint or other visuals that may need a special set up. Always consider the unusual set up need. New technologies may need a new set up.

Be careful not to think that the visual is the key to the presentation. It's not, you are. It's a mistake to dim the lights for long periods of time just so you can show off the newest computer visual. It's also wrong to spend time talking to your visuals. It's your audience that needs your attention. With this in mind, think about the following five steps when using visual aids:

1. Reveal the visual

2. Point to or touch it

3. Turn away from the visual toward the audience

4. Make eye contact with audience

5. Explain the point that the visual supports

Use visuals well and you will increase the level of your presentations.

Q & A

Questions are a part of many presentations. It is important for you to handle them well if they are a part of your presentation.

Keep the theme or purpose of your presentation in mind when answering questions. Try to keep your answers concise and focused on that theme.

When in a large group, repeat each question so that the entire audience can hear it. This will give you time to mentally rehearse your answer. Repeating the question is especially important whenever you get a hostile question. Try to rephrase the question in a more positive manner, a manner that suits your purpose and theme.

After repeating or rephrasing the question, break off from the questioner and make eye contact with the rest of the audience. Too often a presenter will stay in contact with the questioner and engage in a two-way dialogue. Make sure your answers are made to the entire audience.

Be prepared. You will be able to anticipate many of the questions that will come up. Keep your answers short and to the point.

Try to keep your energy up. Question and answer periods need to be thought of as an important part of the presentation, not as a time to relax and let up.

Break down a complicated question into two or three distinct parts, and answer them one at a time. Don't be afraid to say, "I don't know." Don't argue; allow for a few critical remarks.

End the Q & A period on a positive note.

FINAL PREPARATIONS

Avoid last minute panic by dealing with details well before you have to go on.

Confirm where you need to be. Confirm that the equipment you need is in the room and is set up and working. Check the room yourself. If you have a chance to do a dress rehearsal, do one.

Give yourself plenty of time on both the front and back end of any commute you may have. Rushing to get to the presentation, or having to rush through it will not help you be your best.

To be a good presenter requires practice and preparation. It also requires that you be yourself.

18

TIME MANAGEMENT

BELIEVE IT

There are so many demands on your life, and you can expect to have more put on your plate every day. How in the world will you ever be able to manage your time? Most of you won't because you never take the time to determine what makes a real difference in your life.

If you want to manage your time, you must do those things you really value, but will you? Most of you don't believe that you have the control to do so, and so you do a ton of unnecessary activities each and every day. Until you start believing that you have choices on how you spend your time, you will never get control of your life.

Managing your time effectively starts with the belief that you, and only you, can do so. If you don't have that belief, this chapter will not be much help.

PURPOSE AND PASSION

How are you doing? Are you living your dreams? Are you building your life story by doing the things that you have a passion for, or are you letting everyone and everything around you control your actions and your time?

You have reached a position where you are affecting the lives of others, so you already have some terrific traits, behaviors and abilities. Why not go for it all?

In other words, why not try to be one of the few who become extraordinary? To do so requires having a passion to go after a purpose.

Now you may want to use another term than purpose, and there are a lot of good ones to think about (dreams, goals, mission, agenda), but you need to define what it is that you have a passion for, and then go after it. Successful people have a defined purpose, goals and dreams to reach, and are obsessed with the achievement of that purpose.

Identifying your purpose and setting personal goals is the first key to effective time management. I believe your purpose can only be attained when it is supported by activities at work, at home, and at play. Here is a little exercise to help you to start thinking about your purpose.

> You have just turned 80 and you are in excellent shape, and you are having a great time at a party being held in your honor. You have just been presented with a scroll that is a remarkable recollection of your accomplishments and of your character. What would you like included on that scroll?

We don't take enough time to think about ourselves, who we are, what we stand for, and what we can become. But if you have a purpose, and the passion to go after it, you have made an important first step, and it is an important step if you are planning to manage your time well.

PERSONAL GOALS

Research has shown, over and over again, that successful people are goal-oriented. Setting solid meaningful personal goals is a real key to time management, because they will give you clarity and focus when it comes to deciding how you will spend your time.

By doing the 80 year old exercise, you have spent a little time thinking about your purpose, your values and what you want to accomplish. Now is the time to start setting some goals to help you reach that purpose.

This section is similar to the discussion we had in chapter six. The difference here is that we are talking about your personal goals. By setting real personal goals, you are taking a critical step toward time mastery, so let's begin:

1) Goals should be written.

If you want your goals to be clear, write them down. You are much more likely to reach your goals if you have them written out. Now don't worry about being fancy or wordy or having to follow some form, just find a way that suits you. A simple paragraph for each of your 5 or 6 top goals is plenty.

2) Goals should be customized.

Goals should support your personal values. We all have different values when it comes to things such as family, friends, religion, work ethic, recreation, money and even prestige. Whatever you value strongly should be reflected in your goals.

3) Goals should have deadlines.

Keeping goals open-ended is a recipe for failure. To give a goal real meaning and excellent clarity, it must have a completion date put on it. If it is a huge goal with a lengthy deadline, you should break it down into doable chunks, each with its own deadline.

4) Goals should be reviewed and upgraded regularly.

As events, expectations and activities change around you make sure your goals keep up. Goals are never set in stone, so when things change in your life and one of your goals needs changing, change it.

5) Goals should be specific.

Keep your goals simple and concise, and when they become fuzzy, clean them up. There should never be a question as to the result you want to achieve.

6) Goals should be attainable.

There is nothing wrong with setting big scary goals, but make sure you believe you can achieve them. Your mind won't focus on the unattainable for very long, so give it a chance to focus on something that will really make a difference.

7) Goals should be positive.

Direct your goals toward what can be accomplished, not on what should be avoided. There are plenty of negative people who are willing to help us fail to reach our goals, but don't let them. Your mind will focus on the positive if you let it.

8) Don't forget your dream.

Your goals are relevant as long as you are pursuing your dreams. Dream achievement, not goal achievement should always be a priority.

IS IT IMPORTANT?

There are very few success stories that don't include effort and hard work as one of the major contributors. There is little question that you will put a lot of time and effort into your job. You will, however, need to constantly challenge yourself to spend your time and effort wisely.

Everyone can put a list of activities together that will more than fill a day, and the lists of winners and losers contain exactly the same activities. Winners, however, don't try to do everything on the list, while losers do. What winners focus on, and do, are the activities that are important to goal attainment.

Take the time each day to review what is important to you, and do so with an awareness of the activities that will help you reach your goals. Schedule your day around the important activities, and be aware of how you spend your time. It's easy to go off track.

Step back every now and then to evaluate how you spend your time. Be brutally candid with yourself. Ask often:

- What is it that I do that I shouldn't be doing?
- What is it that I am not doing that I should be doing?
- Are the activities and events in my life getting me closer to my goals?
- What is the best way to use my time right now?

URGENCY FACTOR

Humans sure like to spend time on <u>urgent</u> activities. Urgent activities get our immediate attention. And the urgent often receives an undeserved level of importance.

If you are like most everyone else, you probably fall into the urgency trap. But if you are going to manage your time well, make sure the urgent tasks you do are also important. There are so many fun, easy and fast activities that are just not real important, just urgent.

Do the important activities first. Important activities are not always urgent, but they are critical to your success. By substituting some important, not so urgent activities for some urgent, but not so important activities, you are on you way to being a more effective time manager.

The urgency factor is extremely strong, and unless you are aware of how it eats away at your time, it will be a huge reason why you will waste your time.

Identify 4 or 5 things that you do on a regular basis that are urgent, but not real important to your managerial success. Also identify one thing that you don't do, but if you did it regularly would have a positive impact on your managerial effectiveness. Try to do the one good thing by substituting it for 2 or 3 urgent unimportant time wasters. You will find your day to be more productive.

PRIORITIZE

Plan every day to do the important things in your life; in other words, prioritize daily. A good time to focus on your priorities is at the start of each week. Take a few minutes to determine what it is that you would want to accomplish that week and write down a few priorities for the week. Focus on these priorities as you do your "to do" list for the day.

It is easy to schedule activities, but to be successful you must schedule your priorities. Accomplishing activities may fill up your day, but if you fill up your day with low priorities, you will have a day filled with much frustration and little accomplishment.

Each day as you prepare your "to do" list, focus on the activities that are most important to you. Put an "A" next to these items indicating an important task. Review the list for the unimportant but urgent, and identify them with a "D" (for delete). Review the other items on the list and give them "B's or C's" according to their level of importance. As you go through your day, make sure you are spending most of your time on the A's.

Now wait a minute. Not all of you reading the last paragraph agree with doing all that planning, while others think it is imperative. Some of you prefer to be totally planned and organized, while some of you prefer to be very spontaneous. Neither preference is good or bad, but if you catch yourself losing control, it is best to do a little planning.

USE A SYSTEM

There are many tools available to help you with your time management. Day planners, small hand held computers, yellow pads, tickler files, even index cards are effective tools. Just pick one that meets your particular style. As long as the system is comfortable for you, it will be a good system. Find a simple system that works for you, it will help.

COMFORT

Left unto ourselves, we gravitate to our comfort zones. And, if we want to reach our goals, these comfort zones will be a limiting factor.

Take a hard look at yourself and what you do. What you see is often disturbing. You may have to admit that you are not using your time to the best of your advantage, and you will discover that one of the main reasons is that we get into habits that are familiar and comfortable.

If you want to become extraordinary, you must be willing to leave your comfort zones. The ability to grow comes with commitment and resolve, and it is not always comfortable.

DOING IT ALL

There you are writing your "To Do" list and you realize that you have another 20 hour day planned. You can't do it all.

To be a great leader, you have to be brutal with your time. You need to focus on the right processes and the right people. You have to be willing to get rid of some of the events that you did in the past.

Did you ever write a "Not To Do" list? You should. You need to focus on things to eliminate from your day. Being aware that you can't do it all is very important to your success.

TRIPLE A

In summarizing this chapter, three words come to mind: attitude, attention and action.

Your attitude should allow you to dream big and go after your dreams.

Your attention should be on the activities that are important.

Your actions need to be consistent with your attitude and attention.

19

MANAGING STRESS

GOES WITH THE TERRITORY

As you drive to work, do you get that bad feeling in the pit of your stomach? Do you start worrying about the big project due next week, or the presentation you need to make to the boss? Are you worried about the kids? Are you worried about the lawsuit that is pending, or the team member that needs reprimanding? Are you thinking about the rumor that your best team member is leaving to join the competition? And then as soon as you walk into the office, your invaluable assistant comes in with a request for a 3-month family leave. You are overloaded, pass the Maalox.

Problems and hassles will always be a part of your job and your life. Stress is always a part of your life, and if you are not careful, it can cause real problems, both physically and mentally.

It's easy to get caught up in worries and problems, but you must get caught up in a productive manner. Handling stress well is crucial if you want to succeed long term. Research clearly tells us that you can and must manage your stress well if you want to be happy and productive.

GOOD OR BAD

Stress plays a part in everything we do. Loosely defined, stress is the way your body reacts to every activity or situation you are exposed to. Whether stress is good or bad is determined by your reactions and responses to it.

It's wrong to think of stress as negative. As a matter of fact, many of the stressful situations in your life represent a time of joy and accomplishment, and I know you could think of a few right now. Put other people in this same situation and they may see it in a whole different way. What you saw as positive, they may view as negative. It's not the event that causes stress, it's our reaction to the event that is the key.

Think about diving off a 95-foot cliff. To some this would be a wonderful, exhilarating challenge, and to others, a scary nightmare. Same situation, different responses. It all comes down to what we believe is going to happen to us. Stress is personal.

You always have a choice. You can handle stress well by taking a positive attitude toward the situation that is causing the stress, or you can allow the stress to get the best of you. Sounds easy, but it's not.

FEAR

As we evolved, we developed a strong instinct to face the predators of the land. We developed a strong respect and fear of the environment and perils around us. We faced many dangerous situations, and when confronted with one, we would either stand and fight, or take off running. This fight or flight syndrome is still with us today. And fear is still as strong an instinct today as it was thousands of years ago.

Can you think of a time when fear has ever helped you in non-life threatening situations? It doesn't. If fear is stopping you from attempting something that you view as important, ask yourself what will be the worst consequence that will take place if you attempt the situation. All too often, the answer sounds trivial.

You have got to stop fearing things that are important for you to do if you are to going to be successful. You must be aware of when fear is taking over, and stop it on the spot. Awareness and logical reality about the situation are the key.

Learn to love stress. You best accomplishments will usually come during stressful times. Don't avoid it, deal with it.

RELAX

Research has shown that learning to relax is one of the best ways to cope with stress. Relaxation techniques help reduce tension and increase energy.

Autogenic training, developed by Dr. J.H. Schultz, and the Relaxation Response, developed by Dr. Herbert Benson, are two of the more popular techniques. Both get you to quietly relax you body, muscle by muscle. Regular use of these techniques helps your body use its natural stress-combating capabilities.

The most simple of the relaxation exercises you can use is focused breathing. Simply put your hand on your stomach and breathe slowly through your nose. Feel your stomach, not your chest, expand as you breathe in. This is diaphramic breathing and it is the best kind of breathing. As you continue breathing relax your face and shoulder muscles. Feel the tension release from your body.

When you are under stress, you tend to restrict your oxygen intake. Regular diaphramic breathing will help you get all the oxygen you need.

COPING WELL

It's easy to make yourself miserable. Worry a lot, focus on your faults, focus on others' faults, drink too much, never take a vacation, work eighty hours a week, never exercise, and the list goes on and on. There are numerous ways you can bring yourself down. Few are useful, and most are dangerous to your health.

The key to handling stress is to be aware that you are under stress and admit that it is affecting you. You need to identify the stressor, the situation or person causing the negative stress in you, and either eliminate it or do something productive about it. It's your choice, but if you don't replace or eliminate the stressor, it will stay with you.

Here are a few ways to be productive in handling stress:

- Be a goal setter. Write your goals down, and focus on them regularly. Commit to attaining your goals.

- Give yourself a break. Don't be so hard on yourself. Write down your strengths and focus on them regularly.

- Exercise regularly. Keep your fitness level up.

- Review your bad habits—too much alcohol, bad temper, smoking, etc.—Resolve to work on one bad habit at a time. Small incremental wins are terrific.

- Make mistakes and learn from them. It's O.K. not to be perfect.

- Allow others to make mistakes. No one is perfect, and mistakes can be turned into wonderful learning opportunities.

- Balance your life. Invest your energy in more than just your work. Find a pursuit that will energize your life.

- Resolve differences with those you are close to. Meet with them, talk to them, and work together to resolve the problems you have.

Take control over your life. Know your stressors and do something productive about them.

SELF-TALK

If you're like most successful people, you are pretty hard on yourself. Listen to the way you talk to yourself when you mess up. You will probably be putting yourself down, and calling yourself some not-so-nice names. If negative thoughts dominate your thinking, you become very susceptible to self-fulfilling negative behavior and negative stress.

Take a few minutes and focus on your strengths and goals. Write a positive affirmation that supports these two important parts of your life. Focus on this affirmation daily.

Positive self-talk can help, but you need to practice it. Catch yourself the next time you are hard on yourself and turn it to a positive. Being positive is powerful, being negative is destructive.

STRESS CARRIER

Make sure you are not the person causing negative stress on your team members. Do you:

- Fail to listen
- Lose your temper a lot
- Criticize others regularly
- Show impatience
- Act with sarcasm
- Complain to others
- Interrupt others
- Give only negative feedback
- Disagree a lot
- Promise a lot, but don't always follow-through
- Spend little time with my group
- Avoid problems
- Manage upward, while looking down on others

These are all behaviors that cause stress, and they are all too common in the workplace. Know your behaviors, and recognize the effect they have on others. As much as you want to reduce stress in your life, you should just as much want to reduce negative stress in your team members' lives.

20

FADS OR REALITY

FADS

Managers seem to be willing to try just about any new idea that offers a promise of increased profitability or increased efficiency. Most of the ideas are founded in sound theory and make a lot of sense, especially when a convincing consultant presents them. But it's important to figure out which practices are real, and which are not. Let's look at a few.

TECHNOLOGY

Technology has changed the way we think about and do business, and is certainly no fad. Much like the printing press changed the world, so computers will have a lasting effect on how we run our lives.

But we have to be careful and not get caught up in all the hype. The early stages of this great revolution offers so much promise, it's scary. And along with this promise comes many questions. Here are a few of the more negative ones:

- How will hackers increase their sophistication and continue to disrupt and sabotage business ventures and results?

- What happens to the relationship side of human behavior when we tend to go to the computer for the answers to most of our questions and needs?

- How do we know which information is fact and which is fiction?

- What is happening to what used to be private personal information?
- Is technology dehumanizing the world around us?

These are valid questions, and they will sort themselves out. So instead of dwelling on the negative, you need to consider how your area will use technology to enhance, or even dramatically change, what you do every day.

Technology will heighten customer awareness, and allow them to have more choices. It already has commoditized services that were viewed as highly sophisticated. Companies must be proactive in understanding where technology is taking them. Constantly challenge your view of how technology is affecting your business. Constantly focus on your customers, and question how they are viewing technological alternatives.

Products and services are available to us and to our customers 24 hours a day. It's easy to get what we want, when we want it. How are you using the power of technology to enhance your product or service offerings?

Many of the great innovations have changed the way we go about our daily lives, but their perceived impact on the future is often missed. For example, when television came on the scene, it was predicted that the end was near for radio. Nothing was further from the truth. We cannot know which of the predictions will come true about technology, there are so many, but we do know that caring human relationships coupled with enabling technology will be a winning combination.

We all know that technology is no fad. We know that technology is one of the key factors in business today. It's important for you to be a student of technology. This doesn't mean that you become a technologist, but you must have a keen awareness of what technology brings to the table in businesses around the world. Be aware of the trends. At the very least it will be important for you to be completely aware of the implications technology has for your business. You need to continue to learn about its growing capabilities. Spend some time each day reflecting on how technology (the Internet, Biotechnology, Nanotechnology, etc.) is changing the way we work and the way we play.

Technology will not decrease the need for leadership. Technology will demand great adaptability and flexibility from its leaders. The emotionally intelligent leader knows that technology can help drive business. As a result, you must maintain a constant vigilance to be aware of the technologies that will help, and the ones that won't.

SERVICE QUALITY

Every manager will tell you that service quality is important, but there are few organizations that offer real quality service. It's just not easy.

No matter how well you do as a business, people will have certain perceptions about your organization. Some are real, some are not. So part of your problem will be to manage perceptions, and that can be a full-time job. It might be that no matter how good your service is, it might not be viewed fairly. But that is no excuse. You have to overcome any negative perceptions, and it all starts by actually offering top quality service.

There is a lot that you can do as a leader to build a service mentality in your organization. Research is extensive in this area, and gives us lots of data from which to choose. In their book, *The Service Profit Chain*, James Heskitt, Earl Sasser and Len Schlesinger give us a blueprint to profitability and growth. They tell us simply that:

- Profit and growth are linked to customer loyalty

- Customer loyalty is linked to customer satisfaction

- Customer satisfaction is linked to service value

- Service value is linked to employee productivity

- Employee productivity is linked to loyalty

- Employee loyalty is linked to employee satisfaction

- Employee satisfaction is linked to the internal quality of life [11]

And the internal quality of life is linked to you. You are the one who challenges, recognizes and coaches. You are the one who helps employees to reach out and get better. In other words all service quality starts with you, the leader. Your influence has a major impact on client loyalty and quality service.

REENGINEERING

Reengineering is a wonderful idea, but in many cases it has not worked. Why not? Here are a couple of things to think about.

Like many new ideas, managers saw reengineering as **the answer**. They read the books, brought in consultants, and started using the word in all their speeches. On paper it looked like a spectacular idea. And yet it has not been the success that was anticipated. Was it too complicated? Was it too expensive? I don't think so. So what happened?

Like most new "answers," reengineering is a wonderful idea. And like most wonderful ideas, it will work if the leader championing the idea spends as much time working on people issues and change process issues as much they do on the reengineering process issues.

Getting buy-in, managing the resistance the change will foster, framing the change in a way that benefits those who will institute the change, working constantly to get a two way dialogue on making the change a reality, bringing credible evidence to the table on why the change should take place, rewarding change behaviors, empowering the group to improve the process, and so on, is often overlooked when instituting new ideas. In other words, "answers" fail when you put the process over the people. The process will work when you spend your time thinking about how this new strategy will affect those who have to implement it.

It has been reported that reengineering has not worked up to expectations. But no great idea will work unless you focus on the people who have to institute the change. Understanding how the new process displaces old work processes, and the emotional change that occurs when uncertainty and unfamiliarity are introduced, are all key issues when introducing any new "answer."

SIX SIGMA

Six Sigma is often compared to reengineering, but it differs in a couple of key ways. First, it is run internally by highly-trained professionals who have a vested interest in the company's future. Second, senior management is very much involved in project selection. And third, the projects can bring dramatic and often immediate financial results.

Six Sigma does consider the people side in coming up with conclusions. Its methodology and its purpose are clear to everyone involved in the process. It has a chance to be around for a long time.

The DMAIC (define, measure, analyze, improve and control) model when, combined with the "critical to quality" and "defects per million opportunity" concepts, is simple and useable. And whenever you can simplify important work processes, you have a chance for success.

DOWNSIZING/ RIGHTSIZING

This is an example of how the idea from on high makes sense, but often meets resistance from the troops who have to make it work.

Downsizing is an interesting process. On paper it would seem to save the company money, and it would if you could just keep the high performers and get rid of the poor performers. But you don't. In reality you get rid of a mix of the good and the bad. And none of the work goes away.

So what happens? You lose some of the good contributors, people who pulled more than their share, and some weak performers. The work stays the same, or is increased, so the remaining workers have an added burden to an already busy day. The worker works harder, gets things done faster, and puts out more work than ever before. But because there are not enough people to do the work, quality starts to suffer, workers get less recognition, they start feeling bad about their situation and may even start to lose some confidence. And many of the good performers start secretively looking for a job elsewhere.

Downsizing does not mean less work is to be done. It means that the volume of work increases for each worker, and the result is often poor morale. Realize that whenever you downsize, you need to be even more aware of emotions than you normally are. You must be aware of your own emotions, as well as your associates' emotions. You will feel as much of the burden as anyone else, but you must remain positive and focused on the challenges ahead. You must convey this positive feeling by being keenly empathetic to the emotions of those you with whom you work.

Downsizing and rightsizing have played an important part in reducing hierarchies and creating flatter organizations. And getting used to these flatter organizations has to be led by people like yourself, not by some command and control senior manager.

CREDENTIALS

It's amazing how many managers are hiring people for their credentials and not their talents and accomplishments. Credentials look good on paper, but they really don't mean that much. There are so many successful people who have meager credentials, and there are many unsuccessful people who have doctoral degrees.

Be careful when you hire a person with great credentials. The tendency is to give this new person more credence than you give your proven performers. Make sure that performance matches the credentials. Be sure that you never take your proven performers for granted because they have fewer credentials.

Respect those who can do the job. Expect a lot from them. Care for them a lot because of who they are, not for some credential they possess.

IT'S THE PEOPLE

We could talk more about fads, such as TQM, or Management by Objectives, or MBWA, and we could justify why all are solid ideas, but most fail. And the reason why they fail is simple: they fail when you put process over the people.

The practice of management must include the intellect and the emotion. All too often, managers do the intellect part. They come up with practical, objective and logical reasons for their ideas. It is only the great manager who can combine the great logical idea with the impact it has on the people.

Never underestimate the power of people. No process ever works without taking the people into account.

21

WHAT ABOUT YOU?

THE FOLLOWERS

Managing and leading is all about people. If you want people to do a terrific job, start by expecting that they will do well. Then care enough to help them do well. Have the courage to give them both positive and negative feedback. Have the common sense and thoughtfulness to frame things in a way that will get their attention and receptivity.

Become a proactive listener and a keen observer of behavior. Take whatever time it takes to make sure you have an accurate read of your follower's emotions, values, strengths and weaknesses. You must understand what they say, why they say it, and what they really mean.

Never stop paying attention to your followers. Never stop giving them praise. Never stop giving them more to do. Never stop expecting more from them. If you have the right followers and you do right by them, you will find that they will accomplish great things.

BOARD OF DIRECTORS

To be an effective leader, you will need to get solid feedback from your peers, subordinates, superiors and other trusted advisors. Lack of feedback is one of the main reasons leaders derail. If you don't know how your behavior is affecting others, you can go along thinking that things are going well, and be blindsided. Your good intentions may be viewed the wrong way by those with whom you work.

Be careful that behaviors that led to your long-term success don't turn into behaviors that lead to your downfall. For example, you may have gotten great results by pushing others to the limit, and you may have been rewarded with promotions and praise. But if you were just bullying others, there will be a time in your career where your one time "successful" behavior will be the behavior that brings you down. By being aware of your own strengths and weaknesses, you will have the choice to change or to stay the same—but it will be your choice. Being aware of your choices is a real key to emotional intelligence.

So how do you get the feedback you need? One way is to form a personal Board of Directors. Just as corporations receive advice and guidance from a Board of Directors, so can you. Here's how:

> Start by listing people who you respect very much. They can be alive or deceased. They can be famous or just a good old friend. They can be a boss, a relative, a peer, or anyone else with whom you would love to sit down with to get guidance and advice. Just start by putting the names down on paper.

> Now take a look at the names, and choose between three and seven who you know would be willing to give you advice when you need it. Contact them and tell them what you are doing. Invite them to serve on your personal Board. You will be surprised at how honored they are when you ask.

> And then use them. Ask them for advice. Ask them for feedback. Ask them to be tough on you when they perceive a weakness. Listen to them and thank them for taking the time to help you. A good Board of Directors can be invaluable to your development and success.

QUESTIONS ABOUT YOU

There are a number of themes that are repeated throughout this book. The following twenty-five questions reflect these key themes. When your followers answer them positively about you, you will have made it as an emotionally intelligent leader:

1. Are you committed to excellence?

2. Are you giving me a lot of praise and encouragement?

3. Do you give me feedback that helps me improve?

4. Do you care about my career?

5. Do you expect me to do well?

6. Do you have the same high expectations for others in our group?

7. Are you flexible enough to change course when necessary?

8. Do you include me in important decisions?

9. Are you a good communicator?

10. Do you have a vision that excites me?

11. Do you have a great sense of integrity?

12. Are you hiring great people?

13. Can I trust you?

14. Do you listen to me?

15. Do you challenge me with work that I enjoy?

16. Do you challenge me to learn new things?

17. Do your actions match your words?

18. Do you give me credit on a regular basis?

19. Do you handle the tough situation with courage and compassion?

20. Do you adapt to change well?

21. Do you handle the resistance to change well?

22. Are you competent technically, tactically and strategically?

23. Do you get rid of the bad apples?

24. Are you a positive person?

25. Would I want my son or daughter to work for you when they grow up?

Your followers expect a lot from you, and when they can answer yes to each of these questions, you are on your way. One last question:

Would you want to work for you?

SECTION 3:
SUMMARIES AND MODELS

22

EMOTIONALLY INTELLIGENT BEHAVIORS—BULLETED SUMMARY

THE BULLETS

This chapter is different. It's made up of over three hundred ideas taken from the book, all put in a quick bullet type format. The reason for this chapter is to provide you with an area you can quickly go to for ideas and reflection.

It would be great if you have all the time in the world to read and think about the ideas in this book, but usually you are fighting fires or looking for some spare time to return your calls. During your busy day, you may want a quick reminder about negotiation, or coaching, or interviewing, or whatever is next on your day planner.

When you are focused, you usually perform at your best. These quick ideas can help you focus on the task at hand, even when your mind is filled with a lot of important thoughts.

Leading Others

The first step to greatness is to expect great things to happen. Expect the best from yourself. Expect the best from others.

Do your team members a big favor—challenge them to do something great.

Start with a vision of success. Know what winning looks like, and constantly work at communicating a winning vision. Many people are capable of developing a captivating vision that focuses on what is possible, but only a leader can articulate it so that people buy in.

An articulated vision can lead to commitment. Without commitment there is little chance for extraordinary results. Never stop clarifying and communicating your vision.

Visions are simple and emotional. You win people over by concentrating on both the mind and the heart.

A good vision is both achievable and believable because it is easily understood. Form it by taking a practical look at the present, and a flexible look at the future.

Dreamers make good visionaries. Be a dreamer and get others to dream. Walt Disney was one of the best at this. His dreams were extraordinary, as was his commitment to make his dreams a reality. Today the cast at Disney continues to dream and bring us new and wonderful experiences.

What gets focused on gets done. Focus on the results to be attained, and the activities needed to attain those results.

Learn to trust others. Trust starts with you caring, really caring, about others. Leaders care.

Trust others if you expect them to trust you.

The simple fact is if you are not trusted, you are not a leader. Trust does not come easily. It takes time to develop, and it can be lost quickly. Once you earn the trust of your team, you need to constantly work to keep it.

To be trusted you must be sincere and you must be consistent. Give fair feedback to others. Be honest and flexible. Be willing to take risks and accept responsibility. Your behavior must match your words. You must "walk the talk."

Always treat your team members as partners, not as "subordinates." Treating people with respect is a golden rule, and it really works.

Learn the lay of the land. Be aware of the internal and external problems and opportunities your company faces. Be wary of the risks, the competition and the unseen landmines that your industry is facing. Be out front giving guidance and direction.

Emotion is a major part of the game. Leaders work on an emotional, caring level.

Be a learner. Stay on top of the newest ideas and trends in your industry. Encourage your team to surpass you in their industry knowledge. Facilitate meetings in which you and your team can exchange ideas and information.

Be willing to make the tough decision.

Ask others for feedback, and accept this feedback without becoming defensive. Be willing to take a stand when you believe in something, but avoid taking a stand on every issue.

Be willing to accept criticism and admit when you are wrong.

Leadership takes courage.

It takes courage to win—to believe in people—to help them to do something extraordinary with their lives.

Focus on doing what's right, not on what looks good.

Feel good about yourself. Be confident in your ability.

Be careful that your ego does not get in your way as you are dealing with others.

Take responsibility for your own motivation. Help others to take responsibility for their own motivation.

Focus on what is important. Leave the trivial to someone else.

Understand that change is constant. Learn to anticipate and build your expectations on ever changing realities.

Do the right things, not necessarily the popular things. Be persistent in pursuing what is right. The time and effort you put in doing the right things are worth the price you pay.

You can be tough and you can be strong, as long as you care about others. A major study conducted at the Center for Creative Leadership found that being insensitive to others is a major factor in the derailment of managers. No matter how tough things get, and no matter how busy you get, if you fail to pay attention to your people you will lose them.

If your mindset is one of what's in it for me, instead of what's in it for my people, you will have a difficult time gaining their trust and respect.

To really care about a person, try to put yourself in their shoes. Now this is not as easy as it sounds. People's shoes, just like their attitudes, come in all different shapes and sizes, and rarely will they fit you exactly. Working to see things from their point of view as well as your own is critical, and is the starting point for all successful collaboration.

Identify the key leaders on your own team. Ask them for advice, listen to them and act on the good ideas they bring to the table.

Communicate, communicate, communicate and then communicate some more. Share information and encourage your team to share information.

Come down hard on political infighting.

Expect things to be messy, ambiguous and turbulent. Leadership is not easy.

It's followers that make a leader great. Always surround yourself with outstanding people.

Be positive. Focus on the possibilities.

Find ways to make people feel special, make them feel like they are important. Believe in them.

Encourage Change

Expect change to happen. Be positive about change. Look for the opportunity to meet the new challenges and expectations that you are facing everyday. Change is not only part of our life, it is a part that will accelerate in the next few years.

Expect the unexpected. Today change can come out of nowhere.

Understand that all changes both positive and negative will meet with resistance. Encourage people to resist. You can always handle outward resistance.

Keep your goals flexible. Don't become to caught up with past results. Earned arrogance is a deadly disease. Look to get better. Look to learn something that can improve your competence every day.

Study your industry. Know where the competition is coming from. Understand the changing behavior of your client base.

Expect the unpredictable. We don't like the unpredictable because we don't have a sense of control over it. It's uncomfortable for most of us, but it is the reality of change.

Don't expect everyone to fall in line just because you have announced a change. You need to announce, announce, and announce some more. You need to constantly work to get superiors, peers and subordinates to buy-in. Never assume that the change job is ever done.

Build in rewards and consequences to compliment your change efforts.

Help people to get better organized around the change effort. Help them understand the why and how of the change, and why it is important to them. Change happens one "heart" at a time.

Don't confuse action with actual change. People often try the change, not like it, and retreat back to the status quo.

Understand that denial, anger, rationalization and procrastination are all possible reactions to change, Plan to deal with these emotions.

Once you are in control of the current change, expect new changes to be forthcoming. We are working in a time when confusion, innovation, ambiguity and creativity are the norm.

Look for big challenges, opportunities, and problems. Be prepared to go after them with all your energy.

Don't look for the one best answer. It's O.K. to admit you are confused, not certain, or are making mistakes.

Challenge existing practices, no matter how successful they are. Expect a lot of resistance to these challenges.

Change happens when new goals, expectations, resolve, commitment and urgency are the concepts in place. No change takes place when arrogance, status quo, comfort zones, rationalization and denial are the concepts in control.

Hire the Best

Look around you. Some of the best candidates for a job are people working with you or around you. When you have a solid person already working with you, think about them first when you have an opening. Give them a shot at a new job. Believe in them, challenge them, and watch them grow. Don't be blind to the talents of people you already work with.

Know what you are looking for. Identify the skills and qualities that are necessary for a candidate to be successful for this particular job, in this particular culture. Ask your team to give you their thoughts on what they think are the critical qualities of a good candidate. Ask your peers and superiors what they think. Collate all the information and you will have a clear understanding of what a good candidate will look like. **Great hirers will know what they are looking for and will not compromise by hiring someone who lacks the proper skills, qualities, and fit.**

Finding candidates is not always easy. Here are a few ideas to consider:

- Ask your team for referrals. If possible, offer a bonus to a team member who refers a candidate who is hired. You may even carry the bonus idea a little further and give an additional bonus to the team member if the new hire performs to agreed upon level of performance.

- Put a blind ad (an ad with a P.O. Box instead of your company name) in the Sunday edition of a major newspaper. You will get a number of resumes. Only a couple will be gems.

- Hold a career night. Put an ad in the paper three weeks prior to the night, and request resumes be sent to your office. Screen the resumes and invite the ones you like to the career night. Have a speaker talk about your company; give each candidate a brief screening interview and conclude with refreshments. From a night like this you should be able to find some excellent candidates to invite in for a formal interview.

- Talk to the Dean at your local college about setting up an intern program. Setting up a valuable work experience that qualifies for college credit will give you a great opportunity to observe, evaluate and recruit some terrific young talent.

- Join local business associations and clubs. Serve on committees that can lead to valuable contacts. Ask the people at the association for referrals.

- Use the Internet. This powerful tool gets better all the time.

- Ask new hires for referrals.

- Go to the library. Ask your librarian for ideas.

- Look around you. The best candidate may already be in your company.

- Call the personnel department of a company that is downsizing. Tell them what you are looking for, and they may have an ideal candidate.

- Ask your friends for referrals.

- Ask your clients for referrals.

- If you have the funds, use a respected recruiter.

The interview is important. Here are some points to think about:

- View the interview as an opportunity to find someone who can raise the level of your team. Give the interview a lot of thought and energy. Hiring is a privilege.

- Take the first few minutes seriously. After a few minutes of small talk to put the candidate at ease, you should get right to the point. Make your opener short and focused. Let the candidate know specifically what is about to take place.

- Structure the interview into important categories, such as, work experience, education, and activities and hobbies. To help the candidate, it is helpful to put in a transition statement between each category ("Let's now turn to your education…").

- Close the interview by reviewing what will happen next and thank the candidate for coming in.

Leave the candidate with a good impression of you and your company. Even if the candidate is not hired, you want them to say positive things about the way they were treated. You never know who their friends may be.

Try to keep your questions open-ended. If you do ask a lot of closed questions, get in the habit of immediately following up with a series of questions. An example would be:

Closed   - Can you work under stress?

Follow-up   - Tell me about a time when you were under stress?

                 - What did you do?

                 - Tell me more.

- What would you do differently?
- What did you learn from this experience?

Follow up questions are terrific. They will show the real depth of the candidate. Ask a lot of follow up questions. Here are some of the best:

"What else?"
"Tell me more."
"What did you like most about...?"
"What did you like least about...?"
"What did you accomplish?"
"What setbacks did you encounter?"
"What would you do differently?"
"What part did you play?"
"What did you learn?"

If you are ever in the bind for a follow-up question, remember the old stand by questions: Who, What, Where, Why, When, and How.

Keep the candidate focused. Many a candidate will dazzle you with stories about an event or situation, but you need to know about the candidate's behavior and accomplishments, not the event itself. If you catch the candidate going off on a tangent bring them back immediately. Here is one way to do this:

"I seem to have gotten us off track. The situation you are describing is very interesting, but I would like you to tell me your part in the event, what exactly you did. Tell me how you handled..."

Be careful with your questions. Many questions are illegal. Race, religion, color, national origin, sex, physical disability, marital status, arrest records, etc. are dangerous areas to pursue. A good rule of thumb to use when in a danger area is: don't ask the question unless the job requirements make it appropriate to ask.

Be involved in all hiring decisions. Hiring should not be delegated. Every hire is critical.

Watch out for initial impressions, both good and bad. All too often we make up our minds early and spend our interviewing time confirming our initial impression.

Check references.

Prepare for each interview. Know what you are looking for and have a plan for finding it.

Excuse only a candidate's nervousness during the interview. It is natural to be nervous, but never to be rude or inappropriate.

Conduct all interviews in private.

Try to put the candidate at ease. The best interviews are conversational in manner.

LISTEN. The candidate must do most of the talking.

Interview during the part of the day when you are most alert.

Evaluate candidates based on the criteria you set up prior to the hiring process. Don't compromise. Hire the right person because you are convinced they will do a great job.

Listen Well

We all have so many things on our plate occupying our time. Make sure that listening to others is a major part of the menu.

We think about four times as fast as talkers talk. As a result, we tend to focus on the more interesting things floating around in our minds.

Never underestimate the power of listening. When you take the time to listen, you will not only learn a great deal, you will give others recognition by telling them that you care about them. You will make them feel that they are worthwhile and important.

Listening is a critical skill, and yet it is noticeably absent in the workplace. If you take the time to listen, you will stand out as someone who is different. It is the person who listens to employees, competitors and customers who will have a significant advantage in the drive to get ahead.

Be aware of the listening equation:

* The other person speaks   - Words
* Outside interference   - Barriers
* Internal interference   - Filters
* Resulting interpretation   - Listening

WORDS minus BARRIERS minus FILTERS = LISTENING

Catch yourself when your mind goes off and focuses on everything except what is being said. This is a natural act, we all do it. Most people speak at a rate of approximately 125-160 words per minute, but our brain can take in information at a rate of approximately 500-900 words per minute. As a result, we have a lot of time to think about other things while the speaker is talking. Use this time to connect to what the speaker is saying, instead of going off and daydreaming and fantasizing.

Listen for themes, not facts. You can always get the facts later.

Asking questions is a great listening technique, but only if you listen to the answers.

It is more important for the leader to understand the big picture than to be the one who has all the answers. You will get better answers if you are a listener, because when you listen you learn.

Keep an open mind. It is important to know yourself. Know when you close your mind to a particular subject. Admit your tendencies. Be aware of reasons why you are closing off. Are you impatient? Do you have a bias toward this particular subject? Are you upset with the speaker?

Learn to take notes. Experts have found that a listener remembers about 50% of what they've heard immediately after the conversation is completed, and only 25% twenty-four hours later. By learning to keep simple notes, you will be able to raise those percentages significantly.

Don't interrupt. Be patient, you will always have time to get your point in. If you constantly interrupt, you will constantly frustrate others. As a result, they will offer less and less information.

Get beyond the delivery. Not everyone is a great speaker; many have glaring flaws. Great listeners can get beyond the delivery and look for content. This is hard work, but don't give in. Some of the best ideas can come from a bad speaker.

Stay calm. Don't overreact to emotionally charged or inappropriate words. If it bothers you, make a note of it, and make sure you talk to the speaker about it at an appropriate time.

Watch the non-verbals and the tone of the conversation. Studies show that in one-on-one conversations approximately 90% of the message is impacted by the tone and non-verbals. Only 10% through the words.

Monitor your own non-verbals. Good listeners use active non-verbals when receiving a message. Don't be a stone face.

Take an inventory of things in your office that distract you. Get rid of these distractions.

Ask your team to tell you about any bad listening habits you exhibit around them. Work to eliminate these habits.

Listen for the other person's point of view. You have to work to understand what the other is saying because your frame of reference is rarely the same as the speakers.

Overcome your bad listening habits (daydreaming, overreacting, fatigue, impatience, time problems, boring speaker, interrupting, preoccupation, prejudging, etc.). You will be amazed what you will learn. The first step is to be aware of these habits. The second step is to be committed to eliminating the habit.

Learn from everyone. Everyone has something valuable to say. Be respectful to all speakers. You never know when they will add to your knowledge base, or heighten your perceptions.

Be curious. Ask a lot of "why" and "why not" questions.

Use your ears. There is a reason we have two ears, two eyes and one mouth, and yet we tend to overuse the one mouth. When we do a lot of yapping all we do is hear ourselves talking. When we listen and observe, we are learning.

Motivate Well

Give positive recognition as often as you can. People never tire of sincere recognition.

Say thank you often. Handwritten thank you notes are the best. Never miss an opportunity to write one of these notes. They are easy and quick, and people keep these notes because they mean a lot.

Give credit to others for a job well done. Always give credit to someone else. As the boss you will share in the credit anyway.

Celebrate often. Flowers, wine, pizza days, bagels, cider parties or a bottle of champagne all do the trick. It doesn't have to be fancy, but do it whenever you have some achievement to applaud. Spur of the moment celebrations are just as effective as lavishly planned events.

Respect the dignity and diversity of your team. Learn about their needs, values and ambitions. Learn about their family and outside interests. Knowing these things will help you customize something special for them as recognition...It may be something small as a little thank you gift sent to your team members home, but it sure won't be small to the person receiving the gift.

Hold bragging sessions. Encourage your team to talk about their successes. Brag to others about your team.

When you are out of the office, make some calls to your best people to thank them, ask for their advice, or to just say hi.

Hold "whining" sessions. It would be great if everything was always perfect but it's not. Do not be afraid to hear about what is wrong with the way things are working. Encourage people to speak up. Sit around a table and talk about the way things could be better, and give a bottle of "wine" to the person who comes up with the best idea. Keeping resistance hidden does more harm than good.

Never lie. Once you lose your integrity, you will never get it back. Be candid in a sensitive way.

Keep your promises. Don't give lip service. Always keep your word and always follow through.

Admit it when you are wrong. Learn from your mistakes, and allow others to learn from their mistakes.

Set up an advisory counsel. Pick out three or four respected members of your team to give you advice on critical office matters. Listen to their advice, and let them know what actions you will take. Encourage them to inform the other members of your group as to what is being discussed.

Challenge your team. Make sure they have challenging and fulfilling work. Work must be fulfilling if it is to motivate someone to do better.

Compensate others as fairly as you can.

Never take anyone for granted. People need attention. Make sure you are paying the bulk of your time paying attention to your people.

Don't be a phony. People can smell a phony a mile away.

Be Goal Oriented

Superstars set goals. Be a superstar; go after something worthwhile to you.

Be positive. Successful people are "can do" people. They spend their time focusing on goal-oriented activities. Your attitude should be "can do" not "avoid this." Focus on what needs to be done, and on how to get it done.

Be specific. The more specific and clear the goal is, the more likely it will be attained

Write your goals down. Experts say you are 3-4 times more likely to reach your goals if you write them down. When you and your team spend time writing goals, they become clearer and more personal.

Goals should be supported by personal values. People value different things, and meeting individual differences is one of your biggest challenges. Be patient and you will be able to work out goals that are consistent with each individual's values.

Work with your team. Mutually agree upon goals. Setting goals is a two-way street, and it will require a lot of your time, but it will be time well spent. These goal setting meetings are critical. Do them right.

Have deadlines. Dates and times give life to a goal. With deadlines, it is easier to focus and prioritize. Deadlines add a degree of measurement and clarity to a goal.

Upgrade goals regularly. Circumstances change and so should goals.

Set achievable goals. Big stretch goals are terrific if they can be achieved.

Customize all goals. No two people are alike. Everyone on your team will have some common goals, and everyone should also have some customized goals.

Let everyone know what you value and expect. Over communicate your vision for the organization, your dream for your team, the goals for your group, and the expectations for each individual.

Get uncomfortable. It's easy to stay in comfort zones and accomplish just enough to get by. To reach high goals you must make a commitment to leave your comfort zone.

Talk to your team about the dangers of becoming too complacent and comfortable. Challenge them to become and to remain the best.

Get your team focused on what can be accomplished. Help them overcome the fear of failing.

Dream. Real goals are based on dreams. Get people to start dreaming again.

Measure goals whenever possible. Having a measurement you can actually put down on a piece of paper is best.

Be a coach

Observe what's going on around you. Coaching interventions can happen at any time. Be ready.

Use the GAG rule. Try to **Get** the others' viewpoint first. **Acknowledge** what you have heard. Finally **Give** your viewpoint. Avoid jumping headfirst into every coaching situation.

Be specific when giving feedback.

Be timely.

Praise in public, and save criticism for a private place.

Focus on behavior and performance only. As hard as it might be, try to keep personalities out of the coaching intervention.

Describe the behavior observed, and describe the behavior that is desired when improvement is needed.

Be patient. Look at the person's skill, ability, willingness, and experience and customize your feedback at the appropriate level.

Coach the positive as much as or more than the negative.

Be receptive to receiving feedback from your team, your peers and your superiors. Even coaches need coaching.

Over communicate the high expectations and goals you want to reach, and give regular feedback on how everyone is doing.

Listen.

Let your team know how you feel about their progress.

When giving negative feedback, give it and forget it. Never hold grudges. Harping on past mistakes is usually a waste of time.

Try to put yourself in the other person's situation when you are giving feedback to them. Always show them respect.

Give and receive feedback regularly. It is the foundation of leadership.

Don't underestimate the importance of caring. Stay awake for the opportunity to give caring and candid feedback.

Teach Well

Be a lifelong learner first, then you can be a teacher.

People learn best from experiences. Remind your team that the most learning experiences happen on the job. Talk to your people about what they are learning.

Send people to formal training programs. Have them report back to the team what they learned.

Give assignments to team members about the industry, your customers, your competition, or current or future business trends. Ask them to make a formal presentation at your next meeting.

Develop real life mini case studies and discuss them with your team.

Ask one of your best people to become the training coordinator for your team. Work with him or her to come up with a training curriculum that meets team and individual needs.

Ask your team to develop a real life role play. These will deal with people problems and must be handled carefully. You may want to ask the team to simply discuss the situation, or you may want to actually play out the role, and then have a discussion on what took place.

Use games or simulations. Many are on the market today and are specifically geared toward a specific topic, such as teamwork. They usually come with directions for facilitation.

Develop key discussion questions that focus on business opportunities or problems. Facilitate a discussion on the topic. Make sure no one person dominates the discussion, especially yourself.

Prepare. Prepare. Prepare. Training is tough, and to get the proper receptivity level from your group you must always be prepared. If you want training to be taken seriously, you must take it seriously.

Never stop learning. When you stop learning, you stop growing.

Keep building a positive atmosphere. People learn when they can question the assumptions on which their actions are based. They learn little when their mistakes are regularly punished.

Appraise well

No surprises. If you have done a good job of goal setting, analyzing performance, coaching and counseling, and communicating, there should be no surprises at the performance appraisal meeting. An appraisal meeting should simply be a review of what your team member already knows about how he or she performed during the year.

Prepare properly. Gather evidence of performance. Include results achieved, obstacles overcome, recognition notes you may have in a file, and coaching notes you may have. Be as specific and objective as you can.

Pay attention to barriers that may have hurt performance. Be fair. Obstacles may have been beyond the individual's control. Judge these carefully.

Outline the good and bad points to be covered. Determine a fair rating and fill out the appropriate form. Pay special attention to what you write on the form.

Set up the appraisal meeting and don't cancel it. Let the individual know that they should be prepared to discuss their performance at the meeting. Give them a copy of the form you will be using to review their performance.

Know your players and be ready for their response, both positive and negative. Be ready for possible disagreement, emotional outbursts, or misunderstandings.

Listen. If you haven't given a fair rating, change it. Nobody is perfect.

Watch your biases. Be fair. Watch the "halo" effect (exceptional or poor performance in one area skewing the overall rating), and the "recency" effect (recent performance overshadowing earlier performance).

Keep an even keel—some appraisals don't go well. You can't ask people to stow their feelings and emotions. Irrationality can be part of the game. Be ready to deal with it if it comes up.

Build teams

Hire great people if you want to have a great team.

Clarify goals over and over again. Great teams have excellent goal clarity. It is important that team members be on the same page, going after the same goal.

Share information. You cannot over communicate with your team.

Don't allow arrogance. Team members who come in with hidden agendas or feelings of superiority are team breakers and trust busters. You must deal firmly with these people.

Allow only the highest level of integrity. There is no trust without team integrity. Team members need to be open with each other. Strengths and weaknesses must not be glossed over.

Make sure your team stands for something important.

Don't be defensive. Conflict and failure are as much a part of the team process as is success. Conflict resolution requires a candid look at the situation and a lot of solid communication between team members.

Allow others to make decisions. If you make all the decisions you will not foster teamwork. Encourage others to take lead roles on the team, especially when they have the needed expertise.

Be sensitive to the individual needs and expectations of the individual team members. Be supportive, communicate, and always demand high standards.

Be on the lookout for anything that will reduce the trust factor on the team. Trust is critical and tenuous. If trust is lost on a team, there is little hope for exceptional teamwork. Be a problem solver.

Be prepared. Teams can be complex. Team members balance off each other. Changing one element often affects everything a team does. Teams are complex, and with complexity comes opportunity.

Handle Conflict

Expect conflicts to happen. Conflicts take place in the workplace no matter how good you are as a leader.

People are very complex, they come from differing points of view. Take the time to understand others' views. Focus on their differences and their needs.

You can never stop being observant of the things happening around you. Always be aware of how your team is interacting.

Be proactive when you see a conflict in its early stage. Don't let it fester. The earlier you handle a conflict, the less risk of it escalating

Don't fight every battle.

Never overlook the problems that conflict brings and the resulting ripple effect it has on others.

Negativity is a conflict waiting to happen. Don't allow it to fester.

Listen, listen and listen some more.

Don't jump to conclusions.

Maintain your composure. Stay in control even in a heated discussion.

Be realistic. Many of your great ideas will be resisted. Be ready to frame and reframe your ideas. Be ready to change your ideas when appropriate. Don't be the person fueling conflict.

Be a facilitator. Be a mediator. Judge only as a last resort.

Stop blaming and start understanding. There are two sides to every conflict. Question whether or not you are contributing to the conflict.

Take time to focus on the problem—really understand it and you will find it easier to come up with solutions.

Don't assume that someone's intent was bad because a conflict came up. Impact and intent don't always match up. A good intention can lead to a bad result.

Negotiate Effectively

Focus on your needs. Know what you are trying to accomplish and keep your eye on these objectives. Separate your needs from your negotiating positions.

Know your alternatives, they may be better than a negotiated agreement

Keep your emotions in check.

Be patient. Listen. Take your time. Be positive and professional. Keep notes.

Be candid, but don't volunteer too much information early on. Outline your objectives in general terms early in the discussion.

Don't act too smart or be too sophisticated. Ask a lot of questions. Try to get as much information from the other party as you can. Check all information.

Get the other party to state their demands first. Test your opponent. You never know what they may be willing to concede. Always try to get your opponent to make the first offer.

Don't ignore the other party's position, but try to identify their real needs.

Watch the words "but" and "however." Good negotiators use these often, and they can be easily used to get you off track, or comfortable enough to give out valuable information.

Watch the gambit game. Negotiators will employ a number of tactics. These tactics have been proven to be very successful over a period of time. Here are a few to watch out for:

*Good guy/bad guy. This is a very effective tactic even when you know it is being used. Be careful when one opponent is very aggressive and the other reasonable.

*Higher authority. Opponent accepts your offer, but says he needs to take it to a boss or committee for approval. They are likely to come back and ask for a better offer.

*First offer. Jump at the first offer only when it is too good to pass up.

*Take it or leave it. Be prepared to leave it.

*Feel/felt/found. This is a good way to handle objections. "I understand how you **feel**. Many people have **felt** the same way, but what we have **found** with the new research is..."

*Flinch. Good negotiators know the power of non-verbals, and plan for their use. When you make an offer, they flinch. Watch the non-verbals, they may be planned.

*Split the difference. Only do this when it benefits both parties.

*Personal attack. Let the other person vent, but do not allow them to get away with this. If there is a personality clash, you may want to bring another negotiator in to handle the rest of the negotiation.

Know who has the best base of power. Here are some power bases:

* Money. Who has it? Who wants to get it? Is it important?

* Authority. Who has the authority to close the deal?

* Knowledge. How much information do you have? Your opponent? How can you get more?

* Proficiency. Are you the expert? How can you get expertise on your side?

* "Right." Who has "right" on their side?

*Walk-away. Will you be willing to walk away with no solution? Will the other party be willing to walk away?

Do your homework. Listen carefully and calmly. Try to put yourself in your opponent's shoes, but always keep your needs in mind.

Delegate and Empower

Ask people to take on more responsibility. Empowerment is when employees take responsibility without being asked. They learn that they can do this by how you delegate to them in the first place. Good delegation leads to employees who will accept the challenge of empowerment.

Give up control. You will always be amazed at the paradox of the more you give up the more you accomplish. When you delegate, recognize the value of your team member by giving him or her the responsibility, authority, and accountability to accomplish the task.

Evaluate what you delegate. Make sure your team is not wasting their time on the trivial.

Ask your team to help you be a better delegator.

Evaluate your team. Know their strengths and weaknesses and delegate accordingly. Make sure you don't get into the rut of delegating the same type of task to the same person over and over again. They may hate the task, and you are losing an opportunity to give someone else a valuable learning opportunity.

Use any mistakes made as an opportunity to coach and teach. Learning from real life is the best learning.

Give an overall outline of what you want to accomplish, and give the delegatee as much information as possible. Offer to support them in any way they need, but encourage them to make the decisions to bring the project to conclusion.

Find ways to customize the delegation to meet the needs, abilities, and readiness of each delegatee.

Ask the delegatee to summarize the delegation to insure you both agree to the task at hand.

Watch yourself. Don't over control. Establish a follow up procedure and stick to it. Set up a tickler file to remind you when it is the proper time to follow up. Make sure the task or project delegated has a deadline.

Delegate as much in advance as you can. If you are delegating multiple tasks, prioritize them.

Always recognize that the delegation is a time for you to teach, coach and encourage. When you do this you encourage people to take on more work, and eventually they will feel **empowered** to take on more and more responsibility.

Allow mistakes. View mistakes as another opportunity to teach, coach, and encourage. People who fear making mistakes never feel empowered.

Communicate. Be specific with directions and expected outcomes. Give out challenging and worthwhile tasks, especially to your superstars.

Recognize a job well done. Don't miss an opportunity to thank them and give them credit for their accomplishments.

Run Effective Meetings

Don't be the person who continues the tradition of endless and pointless meetings. Hold meetings only when you need to impart critical information, give public recognition, or when the participants will learn something that will help them.

Ask often: "Do we need this meeting?"

Have an agenda. Have goals and priorities for every meeting. Plan your meetings. Try to make them clear, concise, focused and fun.

Avoid the regular meeting habit. There are valid reasons for regular meetings, but challenge those reasons.

Make sure you are not holding a meeting because that is the way you've always done it.

Hold down the number of participants, but make sure you don't leave out a key contributor.

Keep your meetings short. People rarely complain about getting out of meetings early. They will complain about wasted or unproductive time spent in a meeting.

Get your leaders involved. Ask them to help you prepare for the meeting. Ask them to help you run the meeting by being presenters or facilitators. If they recommend that you not hold the meeting, don't.

Distribute the agenda to the participants prior to the meeting. Include the time and place, and any special preparation that the participants will need to do before they attend the meeting.

Find adequate meeting space. Make sure everyone is comfortable. Make sure it has enough space for any equipment you may need, and be sure to order any equipment or refreshments you will need.

Practice any formal presentations you intend to make. Do not wing it. Anticipate objections. Prepare visual aids, and test all equipment.

Prepare handouts, and make sure you have more than enough copies to hand out.

Build in time to recognize others. Give credit to others. Make your meetings a positive experience.

Keep administrative items to a minimum. You can usually cover these in a memo.

Limit interruptions, especially when you are holding meetings in your own office. If you are anticipating a legitimate interruption, tell the group about this interruption at the start of the meeting.

Insist on closure. Summarize key points and key commitments and distribute these to the meeting participants. Brief other interested parties as to the meeting outcomes.

Encourage participation. Get discussion going by using open probes and supporting the responses. Keep asking for opinions, clarification, summaries and examples.

Keep your emotions in check if any conflict comes up. Listen and be patient, and you will be able to deal with any conflict. Try not to use your power as boss. If the conflict is getting out of hand, you may want to table the issue and handle the problem outside of the meeting.

Generate alternatives to ideas. Ask the group for their ideas and record the ideas on a flipchart. Brainstorm and pick the best ideas. Be positive and have some fun.

Terminate When Necessary

No surprises. When your team members get consistent and solid feedback from you, they should not be surprised when they have to be terminated.

Question yourself, but don't second guess your final decision. Firing someone is serious, so always make sure you are right when you decide to terminate someone.

Assemble all the facts you can. Written notices, performance appraisals, complaint letters, coaching notes, etc. are all important.

Prepare information regarding pay, benefits, vacation, or severance.

Plan to give the employee specific reasons on why they are being terminated, and organize these reasons in your mind.

Decide on when and where to have the meeting and schedule it. Avoid Fridays; it is better to have the employee not stewing over a weekend. Never on or near a special occasion (birthday, anniversary, Christmas, etc.).

Plan to be direct and to the point. Plan on how to start and end the meeting.

Be ready for different reactions (knew it was coming, shock, hostility, depression). Don't get into any arguments with the hostile person. Keep calm and stick to the point. With the depressed or shocked person, be patient. Make sure this person understands what is happening, and get them to look ahead.

Leave the person with their dignity in tact. Be straightforward and factual. This just was not the job for them.

Get a partner. Check with Human Resources, Employee Relations, Legal, Employee Benefits or any other part of the organization who may help you work through the termination process.

Make Good Business Decisions

Always think about your customer. Meeting the needs of customers is what business is all about. Always have the customer in mind when making a business decision. Know your customer inside and out, and do everything you can to exceed their expectations.

Take a long view. Always question decision you make because of some short term pressure.

Regularly review your expenses. Make sure your expenses lead to customer satisfaction. Don't let fat sneak into your area. Everyone knows how hard it is to get rid of fat.

Be aware. Maximizing profitability is part awareness and part common sense. Look around and observe how things are being done. Reflect on how fast things are changing, and what you are doing to keep up. Focus on what is working well and what needs improvement.

Become an expert in your business. Know where your costs and revenues are coming from. Know your competition, and how you stack up against them.

Review any Profit and Loss statements you may get as a manager. Learn what is on the statements. Have a line by line knowledge of any statement you may be receiving. Review these statements regularly, even when you delegate them to someone else. Look for trends or mistakes, the statements can tell you a lot. Get copies of previous years statements and compare them with your current statements.

Share your business results with your team. Ask them for help in making these results stronger.

Learn how to budget. Make the budget real, and monitor it. Revise it when appropriate.

Get a partner. Ask a respected peer to sit down with you and go over your statements. Share ideas with each other on how to do things better.

Run your area as if it was your own business and you should make good business decisions.

The client, whether he or she is an internal or external client, is the reason we are in business.

Presentation Skills

Being nervous before a presentation is normal. Often nervous presenters make a solid presentation. Don't let nervousness stop you. Visualize success.

If you want to be a great presenter, customize each presentation to each unique audience. Always customize your presentation with the unique audience you are presenting to. Remember, all audiences are unique.

The number one presentation skill is eye contact. Great presenters look directly into the eyes of their audience. Focus on one person for a few seconds and then go on to another person. This is the one skill you must master to be a good presenter.

Watch your non-verbals, they are important. Gesture naturally.

Slightly bend your arms at the elbow. This little move will help you to gesture well.

Take a lot of deep breaths. It will help you get the needed oxygen you need to put energy into your presentation.

Movement is good, especially when you move in and out of the audience. But excessive movement will distract your audience.

Record your voice; nothing is worse than a monotone presentation. Make sure you modulate.

Practice/ Practice/ Practice.

Videotape yourself. Look for your best traits. Eliminate only those negatives that are distracting.

Organize your presentation. Fill it with stories, anecdotes, analogies, and even a few statistics.

Always practice a good opening and a good close. They will serve you well.

Prepare visual aids to support your presentation. But remember, you are the presenter, not your aids.

If you are going to allow for questions and answers, prepare for this session.

Be focused, be prepared, be concise.

Remember the audience. Connect your message to them or your presentation will fail.

Be a storyteller. Great presenters tell stories.

Manage Time Well

Clarify your goals. Going after meaningful goals is the key to time management because they lead to self-management. Successful people are obsessed with the achievement of their goals. They spend their time on goal-oriented activities and events.

Write your goals down. Review and update them regularly. Make sure they are personal, attainable (not necessarily easy), positive and specific. Make sure they have deadlines.

Evaluate how you spend your time. Be honest. Ask often; What is it that I am doing that I shouldn't be doing? What is it that I am not doing that I should be doing? Are the activities and events that take up my life getting me closer to my goals?

Watch the FEQ's (fun, easy and quick). There are many activities that fall into this category. Many FEQ's are trivial and waste a lot of time. Eliminate one or two of these FEQ's from your routine every week.

Do the important things first. Important things are not necessarily the most urgent, and the most urgent are not necessarily important. We tend to do the urgent, even when it is trivial. This "urgency factor" is extremely strong, and unless we work to focus on doing what is important it can cause us a lot of time problems.

Plan and prioritize daily. Each day prepare a daily "to do" list. Be careful that you are not just filling the page with a lot of activities. Fill the page with your priorities, the activities that will help you attain your goals.

Use a system. Any system, day planners, computer planners, yellow pads, index cards, tickler files, can be effective as long as you can keep track of how you are spending your time. Keep your system simple, and customize it according to your needs.

Focus on what is important to you. Leaders spend a lot of time on things that are important, such as hiring, teaching and coaching.

Leave your comfort zones. It is easy to get into a comfortable routine and stay there. Leaders are willing to take a hard look at their behavior, and leave their comfort zones in order to achieve great things.

How you spend your time says everything about you. How do you spend your time?

Handle Stress Well

Give yourself a break. Stress is a part of everything we do. Our reaction to every activity or situation is what causes stress, both good and bad.

Be positive. We always have a choice. We can handle stress by taking a positive attitude, or we can let the stressor get the best of us. Sounds easy, but it's not.

Don't be so hard on yourself. Focus on your strengths. Be aware of your reactions, and which ones give you the most problems. Be realistic and don't sweat the small stuff. And if we put things in perspective, almost everything is small stuff.

Admit it when you are under distress. Identify what the stressor is and either eliminate it or do something productive about it.

Exercise regularly. Have an outlet. Keep your fitness level up.

Always try to improve your mental ability. Look for ways to learn. Read a book on coping with stress and apply some of the techniques described (relaxation, proper breathing, visualization, biofeedback, etc.).

Review your bad habits. Too much alcohol, smoking, bad temper, or too little rest can all cause negative stress. Resolve to work on resolving one habit at a time. Small incremental wins are a terrific way to combat stress.

Allow others to make mistakes. Allow yourself to make mistakes. No one is perfect, and mistakes can be great learning opportunities.

Balance your life. Invest your energy in activities beyond work. Find a pursuit that will energize and challenge you.

Resolve differences with people you are close to. Meet with them and ask them to help you work through the problems you are having.

Practice positive self-talk. Catch yourself next time you are criticizing yourself and turn it to a positive. The more positive that you become, the less negative stress you are likely to encounter.

23

EMOTIONAL INTELLIGENCE MODELS

What About You

The importance of leadership has been emphasized for centuries. What makes up a leader in the past and what makes up a leader in the future will look much the same when you put the traits on a piece of paper. Courage, attitude, self-confidence, focus, discipline, passion, vision, energy are all wonderful traits, but what do they really mean for you as you develop as a leader? Think about yourself, do you have these traits?

In order for you to grow as a leader you must be a learner. You need to continually be aware of how you behave and how you come across to others. You need to acquire new skills to adapt to new situations.

Competency Model

We recently facilitated focus groups with over 400 managers and came up with many different ideas and thoughts on leadership. The most common themes can fit in a simple, yet powerful competency model. Here it is:

1) Vision

- Defining reality

- Shaping strategy to provide meaning to your staff

- Being aware of your own strengths and weaknesses, and look to others to fill in the gaps
- Being reflective, learning from experience
- Being open to feedback
- Being open to new perspectives
- Dream and get others to dream

2) High Expectations

- Being results oriented, with a high drive to exceed objectives
- Raising the bar
- Being an expert at working through change, and changing expectations
- Building a relationship one on one
- Setting challenging goals and taking calculated risks (one on one)
- Persisting in seeking goals despite obstacles or setbacks
- Operating from a positive view rather than from a fear of failure

3) Caring

- Showing sensitivity and understanding to other's perspectives
- Helping others by understanding their needs and feelings
- Respecting and relating well to people from varied backgrounds
- Fostering open communications
- Listening well, seeking mutual understanding
- Being effective in give and take, registering the emotional cues in attuning the message—seeing the invisible

4) Learning/Teaching/Coaching

- Being open to new ideas
- Being a student of change
- Being flexible in how to see events

- Building trusting, empathetic relationships

- Getting others to see how things really are and working with them to reach their full potential

- Acquiring new knowledge and helping others to pursue continuous learning

- Helping others with the "how to" change and grow

5) Empower

- Helping others reach their full potential

- Taking risks associated with letting go

- Showing vulnerability

- Delegating important tasks in order to get more done

- Understanding that really empowering others is critical to winning

- Having the right people to empower things to is critical. Be aware of constantly upgrading the talent in your office

Think about yourself. How does your behavior fit in with the different competencies? Where are you strong? Are there any weaknesses that stand out?

The competency model above is probably similar to other models you may have seen, and no model is perfect. But if you use the model to think about yourself and what you need to do to develop as a leader, it will be helpful.

The Emotional Behavior Model

Since this book has been about behavior, the emotional intelligence model offered should also be about behavior, so here it is (the model is depicted on page 196):

Explanation

The model starts with you taking a look at your own behavior without judging it. Now this isn't easy because we have a tendency to judge everything we do. But in order to increase your emotional intelligence you must be able to catalog what you actually do, not what you meant to do. If you look at your natural filter of judging what's right and what's wrong, you will never really see your true behavior. Your rationalization filter will take over and you will tend to justify what you have done. So start by being candid with yourself, and what you are actually doing.

After cataloging what you actually do, judge it. Ask yourself the questions in the boxes surrounding the model, and spend a few minute thinking about how your behavior and emotions are helping or hurting your effectiveness.

Think about the people you work with, and how their behavior and emotion affects the work environment. Consider how you might help them emphasize their strengths and minimize their behavior so that they can achieve their goals and dreams. Remember, feedback is the foundation of leadership, so add value everyday by helping your associates learn and grow.

Finally, take one more look at yourself. Consider how your own control or lack of control over your emotions is affecting your behavior. If you can control your own emotions, you will be better at helping others achieve extraordinary results. The person who is constantly flying off the handle will drive fear into his or her subordinates and get compliant results (not necessarily bad results).

The underpinnings of this model are critical. In order to be emotionally intelligent, you need to have courage (the ability to do the right thing for the right reasons all the time), resilience (the ability to constantly pick yourself up when you get knocked down), communication skills (the ability to connect with others), empathy (to really care), and presence (to do what you say you will do, and to be positive even in the face of reasonable negatives).

So what does the model say about you. One thing is certain—no one has too much emotional intelligence. It's something we can all get more of.

Your Legacy

Who are your mentors, the people who have helped you become the person you are today? What is it about these people? Why did you put them on your list?

- Did they believe in you more than you believed in yourself?

- Did they care enough to give you proper advice and guidance when you needed it the most?

- Were they there for you in good and bad times?

- Did they trust them?

- Did they trust you?

- Did they encourage and even push you to be better, even extraordinary?

- Were they people who made mistakes along the way—were they real?

These are interesting questions to me, and the questions you may think about could be totally different. But we all put people who are or were special to us on our list of mentors. Part of the legacy they leave in life will be the success they had in helping you.

Whose list do you make? I believe emotionally intelligent people do many of the things mentioned in this book, and as a result make a difference in people's lives. I believe that with a little work and awareness, everyone can do these behaviors. I also believe that many of you will help someone to do something extraordinary in his or her life. And when you do, you will leave a legacy that is important and will be remembered.

What will your legacy be?

Emotional Behavior

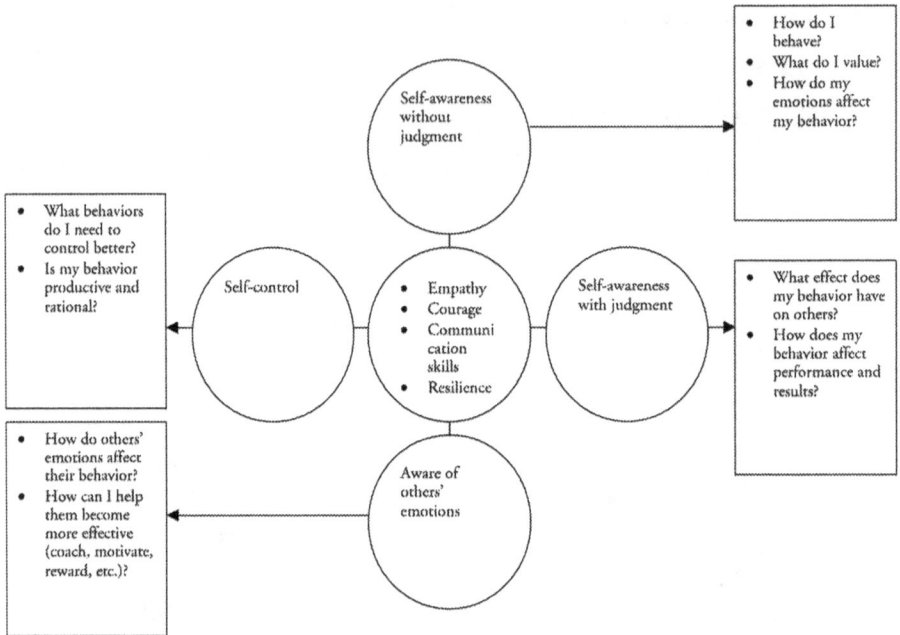

NOTES

1. Goleman, Daniel, *Working with Emotional Intelligence* (New York, Bantam Books, 1998) 317-318.

2. Tichy, Noel M. and Cohen, Eli, *The Leadership Engine* (New York, HarperCollins Publishers, 1998) 51.

3. Bennis Warren, and Nanus, Bert, *Leaders* (New York, Harper & Row Publisher, 1985) 65-66.

4. Conger, Jay A., *Winning 'Em Over* (New York, Simon & Schuster, 1998) 138.

5. Kouzes, James M., and Posner, Barry S., *The Leadership Challenge* (San Francisco, Jossey-Bass Publishers, 1995) 15.

6. McCall, Morgan, W., *High Flyers* (Boston, Harvard Business School Press, 1998) 52.

7. Schwarzkopf, Norman H., *It Doesn't Take A Hero* (New York, Bantam Books, 1992) 168-169.

8. Larson, Carl E and LaFasto, Frank, M.J., *Teamwork* (Newbury Park, CA, Sage Publications, 1989) 27.

9. Fisher, Roger and Ury, William, and Patton, Bruce, *Getting To Yes* (New York, Penguin Books, 1983) 97-106.

10. Mehrabian, Albert, *Silent Messages* (Belmont CA. Wadsworth Press) 75-80.

11. Heskett, James L. and Sasser, W. Earl and Schlesinger, Leonard A., *The Service Profit Chain* (New York, The Free Press, A Division of Simon & Schuster, 1997) 20-21.

ABOUT THE AUTHOR

Tim McManus has led a life filled with leadership experiences. He has been a winning coach, president of a number of different organizations, a board member of a foundation for premature babies, and was even a Drill Sergeant in the Army (although an easy one).

In the world of academia, Tim taught at both the high school and college level. He was a successful high school coach and administrator.

In the business world, Tim spent three years at Coopers & Lybrand in their Professional Education Group, and twenty years with Merrill Lynch in their Management Development Group—the last six as Director of Leadership Development.

In 2004, Tim and his wife Jan moved to Ponte Vedra Beach, Florida. In 2005, Tim formed a new leadership development company called McManus Associates.

978-0-595-36740-5
0-595-36740-2